P9-DHI-286

The Church or the Bible?

H. J. Marshall
Aug. 1993

Publisher's Cataloging in Publication
(Prepared by Quality Books Inc.)

Marshall, H.J., 1943-
    The Church or the Bible? / by H.J. Marshall.
    p. cm.
    Includes index.
    Preassigned LCCN: 93-91524.
    ISBN 0-9636743-4-X

    1. Catholic Church--Doctrines--History.   I. Title.

BX1474.M37 1993   230.042
                                   QBI93-1000

The Church or the Bible?

by

H. J. Marshall

MARSHALL PUBLISHING COMPANY
Boothwyn, PA

PUBLISHER'S NOTE

To ensure the accuracy and completeness of the information contained in this book, all sources have been exhaustively researched. However, neither the author nor the publisher assumes responsibility for any errors, inaccuracies, omissions, or inconsistencies contained herein. Failure to recognize any particular person or denomination in a perspective appropriate to their stature is not intentional. Readers should exercise personal judgment regarding the views expressed in this book and are encouraged to seek any authoritative person or source for specific enlightenment.

© 1993 H. J. Marshall
All rights reserved

ISBN 0-9636743-4-X
93 Library of Congress Catalog Card Number 91524

Marshall Publishing
Boothwyn, Pa. 19061

Printed in the United States of America

Dedicated to my mother
Agnes M. Dewees
October 28, 1910 - November 7, 1985
The Years of the Comet

Words to remember:
"Whatever you feel you would wish for at your dying hour, do now."

Acknowledgments

Rev. James E. Cahill, C.M., Confraternity Home Study Service
Rev. William Jones
Catholic Information Service
Franciscan Sisters of St. Elizabeth
Daughters of Charity, St. Vincent de Paul

Acknowledgments of these books in the public domain

The Nicene and Post Nicene Fathers,
    William B. Eerdmans Publishing Co.
Essay on the Development of Christian Doctrines,
    Cardinal Newman
Beautiful Pears of the Catholic Truth (1897), Eminent writers of
    Europe and America
Grounds of the Catholic Doctrine, Pope Pius, IV
The Blessed Sacrament, Cardinal Manning
The Teaching of the Twelve, B.F.C. Costelloe, M.A.
St. Antony of Padua, C. Kegan Paul
The One True Church, Rev. Arnold Damen, S.J.
The Mass and the Sacraments, Martin Luther

Contents

Chapter 1
Tradition

Before I discuss individual doctrines that separate Catholics and non-Catholics, I would like to show the negative manner in which some anti-Catholics try to discredit the Catholic faith. So much can be distorted by them that anyone may be confused. To help you understand Catholic tradition first, there are man-made traditions which may change in time (not to be confused with sacred traditions which came from God). Sometimes Protestants will focus their sermons on Catholic tradition without an accurate distinction. My desire in writing this book is to educate all those who want more information about what they believe and why they should believe it.

Unfortunately, some anti-Catholics sincerely consider their own feelings as a valid assessment of Catholic tradition. It is sad to say the use of their best speculation is not the best answer. As one example, I note the attacks on the use of candles; these same attacks were answered over a thousand years ago by Jerome in *Against Vigilantius*:

> They should remember the Scripture for even the Apostles pleaded that the ointment was being wasted, but they were rebuked by the voice of jesus. Jesus did not need the ointment nor do the saints and martyrs need the light of candles; and yet that woman poured out the ointment in honor of Christ, and her heart's devotion was accepted. All those who light these candles have their rewards according to their faith.

Yes, there are Christians who have the audacity to claim Catholics are idolaters. This is the consequence of the Catholics' not agreeing with them. But are they forgetting what the Apostles said: "Let every one abound in his own meaning"?

There is one outspoken accuser of the Catholic Church, the TV evangelist Jimmy Swaggart. He has written a complete book, *Catholicism & Christianity*, to discredit the Catholic faith and all its doctrines, beliefs, traditional customs, and rituals. He and his book are so ludicrous that the Catholic Church does not even bother to answer him. But I would like to make a few comments concerning his errors. In his book, he tells us that infant baptism first appeared in Church history around the year 370 A.D. Obviously, he never heard of the Great Origen, a student of Clement of Alexandria, for he said in the second century, "The Church received from the Apostles the tradition of giving baptism to infants."

The Catholic Church will use as supportive evidence of its belief in Purgatory ancient grave inscriptions on tombs. But according to Mr. Swaggart, ancient tombstones bear only the inscription "I sleep." It seems this religious teacher is looking in the wrong places, for he did not see the graves of Abercius of Hienoplis (before 216 A.D.). It reads, "He who understands this, let every Co-religious utter a prayer for Abercius."

Frankly, Mr. Swaggart, before you make any more public condemnation on doctrinal differences or publish your own judgmental errors, think! If Catholics wish to give honor to the Blessed Mother, "All generations shall call me blessed", and you wish to refer to her as a poor peasant girl, why argue about personal opinion? We all worship God.

Read what John Newman, the well-known British Cardinal, had to say about the Catholic Church:

> The Christianity of the second, fourth, seventh, twelfth, sixteenth, and intermediate centuries is

in its substance the very religion which Christ and His Apostles taught in the first.

And this one thing at least is certain; whatever history teaches, whatever it omits, whatever it exaggerates or extenuates, whatever it says and unsays, at least the Christianity is not Protestantism. If ever there were a safe truth it is this. And Protestantism has ever felt it so. I do not mean that every writer on the Protestant side has felt it; for it was the fashion at first, at least as a historical argument against Rome, to appeal to the past ages, or to some of them; but Protestantism as a whole, feels it, and has felt it.

This is shown in the determination already referred to of dispensing with historical Christianity altogether, and of forming a Christianity from the Bible alone: men would never have put it aside, unless they had despaired of it. It is shown by the long neglect of ecclesiastical history in England, which prevails even in the English Church....To be deep in History is to cease to be a Protestant.

Are men such as Mr. Swaggart so misinformed, or is there a definite prejudice against all who will not accept what they say? Some will lead you to believe that they act with the authority of the Holy Spirit, making claims that God has revealed this and that to them, and to them only. To them I give this advice from St. Teresa of Avila, who warns us against such desires of visions and revelations. First: there is a lack of humility with these desires and great perils from the devil can occur. Second: when a person has a great desire for something, he persuades himself that he is seeing or hearing what he desires.

Evidence of Tradition

The Catholic Church retains its ancient historical writings from the time of the New Testament. These records are the letters of the Apostolic Fathers. Many of them, like the Apostles, gave their life for Christ. Their testimony was usually firsthand from the Apostles, or from someone who listened to the Apostles. This is a tradition we received and an interpretation of the Bible. There is no question as to the sources' reliability. If any of the ancient writings of the Church were to hold an erroneous doctrine, it would have been condemned at once.

Listed below are the writers to which I will refer most often:

First, Second, and Third Centuries

Clements (?-97 A.D.)	Bishop of Rome
Ignatius (?-107 A.D.)	Bishop of Antioch
Polycarp (69-155 A.D.)	Disciple of John
Justin (100-163 A.D.)	Christian writer
Irenaeus (120-203 A.D.)	Bishop of Gaul
Tertullian (160-? A.D.)	Christian writer
Origen (185-251 A.D.)	Scholar and teacher
Cyparian (200-258 A.D.)	Bishop of Carthage

Third, Fourth, and Fifth Centuries

Eusebius (260-340 A.D.)	Church historian
Cyril (315-386 A.D.)	Bishop of Jerusalem
Gregory (332-398 A.D.)	Bishop of Nyssa
Ambrose (340-397 A.D.)	Bishop of Milan
Jerome (347-407 A.D.)	Biblical scholar
Augustine (354-430 A.D.)	Bishop of Hippo

Some Protestants publicly challenge the Catholic Church to demonstrate that the early Christians of the first three centuries accepted the same beliefs that are accepted today in the Roman Catholic Church. Although I cannot speak for the Catholic Church (I am but a lay Catholic; I am searching and finding answers to my faith,) I do my best to answer these challenges. To understand the Church, you must understand the changes that have taken place. For example, the early Church practiced public confession, and gradually it changed to a more personal and private confession. Therefore the sacrament always existed but in a different way. And we know that the sacrament existed from Eusebius' Church history: "Gordianui, a Roman emperor (238-244), was not permitted to enter church until he had made confession and occupied the place of penance."

Irenaeus (120-203 A.D.) is another example of the tradition received from the Apostles. His work *Against Heresies*, written between 182 and 188, is one of the most precious remains of early Christian antiquity. It is a defense of the Catholic faith, shedding light on the doctrines as well as the practices observed by the Church of the second century. He writes of the dignity of Rome:

> The greatness of Rome, that is, as the capital of the Empire, imparts to the local Church a superior dignity, even as compared with Lyons, France, or any other city church. Everybody visits Rome: hence you find there faithful witnesses from every side (from all the churches); and their united testimony is what preserves in Rome the pure apostolic tradition.

It should be noted that orthodoxy was indeed preserved there, just as long as Rome permitted other churches to contribute their testimony, like that of Irenaeus, and thus to make her the depository of all Catholic tradition, "by all, everywhere, and from the beginning" (Irenaeus).

Why Catholics Accept Tradition

First it must be understood that all who believe in their Church do so by faith. Catholics who remain faithful do so by trust in their Church, which is based upon the Word of God, tradition, and historical evidence. By faith, we accept the Catholic Church with its knowledge of all past ages, to teach us the truths handed down through Jesus and His Apostles. And those truths can be found in our Apostles' Creed. As an added thought, Catholics accept the teaching authority of their Church, because it would be useless to exchange scriptural quotations with others who have difficulties with Catholic teachings. So what one needs is this teaching authority, which sheds light on problems of doctrinal difficulties. For example, some non-Catholics do not believe in Purgatory, and their only reason is that it can not be found in the Bible. This is simply because their Bible does not contain *Maccabees* as does the Catholic Bible. Tradition is also rejected, even though it contains reliable, authentic, historical accounts of ancient beliefs. This ancient belief can be found in many ancient writers such as Tertullian (160-240). He writes: "The faithful wife will pray for the soul of her deceased husband, particularly on the anniversary date of his death."

Anyone can see the impossibility of discussing Bible quotes with someone who has a different Bible and rejects tradition.

Chapter 2
The Church or the Bible

Who was Appointed to Teach?

Of course, the answer is obvious. In the beginning, there was no Bible, and men were the teachers of the new Christian religion.

This book is not only for the enrichment of Catholics, but also for our separated brethren, who, by personal examination, can understand us better. There are some outside the Catholic Church who have been taught to despise and hate us. You can learn what the Catholics teach and why it is taught. You can test for yourself by the principles of truth, if our arguments are rational and logical. I would like to make the point that I am not trying to criticize others, but to defend Catholics' right to worship as they have through all generations. So, judge us not by false assumptions of others.

First Principles

The great majority of our separated brethren wish to be fair to Catholics. They are considerate of the false and distorted views of others and accept our way of worship and acknowledge our beliefs. They may even study our doctrines but cannot accept them because of belief in their own principles. Our doctrines may run counter to their beliefs, which they assume to be correct. Their aim is to be honest and nothing more. This attitude deserves our deepest respect.

"Truth held without proof" is to all of us a first principle. Just what are first principles? When someone asks a question, you begin with a series of "becauses" and come to the last "because," which is the principle you base all others on, and for which you have no proof and need none, because to you it's self-evident through faith. Each of two who differ starts from his own principles, which are taken for granted.

The Catholic Church has its own first principles, and so does Protestantism have its first principles, and we each acknowledge the right of the other. But Protestantism has no right to judge Catholic doctrines by Protestant first principles, as if they were absolutely certain. They cannot be absolutely certain, since they are denied by Catholics. The Church cannot be judged by any one rule. To begin with, Catholics and Protestants have their own separate rules of faith. Catholics believe that the Bible is not the whole of God's revelations. *The Apostles left behind them a number of doctrines not in writing, but living in the mind of the church.* Protestants deny this, as for argument's sake they have a right to. But they have no right to assume their contrary assertions are true without proof, and to use them as truth is foolish.

Protestants consider the Bible as the only basis of discussion. This is their first principle. Proof is in Scripture alone, they believe. See how useless it would be to argue with someone about rituals when he does not agree with you in the principles that form the basis of rituals? But what has he done? He has judged rituals not by our principles, but by his. First principles are a frequent cause of misunderstanding between Catholics and non-Catholics. It is called false assumptions.

There are no reformers who can base their separations and their teachings on proof. The main reproach against theologians of the Catholic Church was the employment of their own arguments and rational evidence to justify divine revelation. Luther appealed to the Bible alone, Calvin to predestination, Crammer to royal supremacy. Their arguments rested on their individual assertions and were not founded on reason or rational proof. So, let me call your attention to that of which many are unaware. Their judgment of the Catholic Church is founded on prejudice and assumptions. So be alert to those who criticize. They will do their best to analyze and discredit your beliefs. They will attempt to expose and disprove your principles by their own first principles, not by yours, which is against logic.

The Church as Teacher

The true Church was appointed by Christ to teach all nations. Christ set two conditions for salvation: baptism and faith. "He that believeth and is baptized shall be saved." Without hesitation, we must believe all that He taught, upon the authority of God. Catholics accept all of God's teachings through the apostles and their successors, in all ages.

We must, therefore, believe what God commands us to do, and God must give us the means to know. It must be within the reach of the people until the end of time. God's teachings must be infallible in His Church, so we may be without the fear of error. They cannot be the Bible with private interpretation—that has been the teacher of Protestantism—but the Church of the living God.

If God wanted us to learn His religion from a book, or Bible, He would have given it to us. Instead, He sent His Apostles and priests throughout the world. "To teach all nations, baptizing them and teaching them to observe all the things I [God] have commanded of you."

No, Christ did not say to His Apostles, "Sit down and write Bibles and give them to all the people and let every man read his Bible and judge for himself." Can you imagine the confusion of the resulting religion and Church? Just that happened through the reformers of the sixteenth century and we have seen the results.

The Catholic or "Universal" religion had already existed 65 years before the Gospels were written. How did these first Christians know what they had to do to be saved? They knew it in the same way the Catholics know it today: by the teachings of the Church. There were false Gospels during the time of the early Church, such as the Gospel of the Infancy of Jesus, the Gospel of Nicademus, of Simon, of Barnabas, of Mary. Of all these Gospels circulating, who was to know which were inspired and which were false? For three hundred years there was no Bible for guidance. Who was to know whether the Gospel of Luke or the Gospel of Simon was to be included in the Bible?

In the fourth century, Bishops from around the whole world gathered together and assembled in a council to decide which books would make up the Bible as we have it today. This Bible was to be the complete word of God (except that the Protestant Bible removed some books).

And for 1400 years, the Christians were unable to read the Bible until printing was invented. These sacred books were very costly and rare. There were many Christians martyred for the faith who had never seen a Bible. It is not likely that Christ would have left the world without instructions for that length of time if the Bible were necessary for mankind's salvation.

Let us suppose that we have a faithful translation of the Bible from the Greek and Hebrew texts. As such, it is the infallible word of God and it is the foundation of our religion and our guide to salvation. It will be up to you by private interpretation to believe without a doubt all that you read in it. Around the world, there are hundreds of denominations of churches, and all of them say the Bible is their guide. Sincere as they may be, all feel they are the true church of God. This is impossible, since truth is one as God is one and there cannot be any dispute about the word of God.

The Catholic Church is also universal in its Apostles' Creed. The Protestant denominations are made up of contradictions amongst themselves, and in some cases even amongst their own churches. One church will teach that you must be baptized by sprinkling; yet another will say you must go down to the river like Jesus. One will say you have no religion at all until you feel the Spirit of God moving within you. Some say baptize only adults; others say babies, also. Some Protestants are guided only by reason and judgment. Once church will say there is no Hell. Also, we hear you don't have to be baptized at all and it can be proved by the Bible. Another will say you must baptize the men and not the women. From some we hear that if you want to go to Heaven, my friend, you must work out your salvation in fear and trembling. So, "Shake my brethren, shake and be saved."

Some denominations will preach predestination: those whom God selects for salvation, and damned be the rest. Others preach "justification or salvation by faith alone." Do this in remembrance of Me," can be interpreted in many ways by Protestants. Some accept the real presence of Christ in the Eucharist. Others say it is only a memorial. Almost all accept the doctrine of the Trinity, but the Unitarians, they deny Christ was God. The Quakers have no creed. All rests with the individual. Baptism may be a sacrament to some or a symbol to others. It can be a sacrament, but without grace. Spiritual authority is accepted by some and denied by others. Some churches want total liberty to teach and interpret the Bible as they understand it.

Who then is the teacher of the Bible? He who has the true meaning of the Bible! But, the Bible does not tell us who that is. The Bible is not the teacher. It is the word of God and the inspiration of God written down by men. The Bible does not explain itself and one's private explanation is not divine inspiration. It may be a personal understanding, but one can't pretend to be inspired. The Catholic Church teaches the Bible is the word of God and that God has appointed an authority to guide us as to the true meaning of the Scripture. I believe the Church because I believe God has commanded me to believe the Church. Christ said: "Hear the Church and he that does not hear the church let him be to thee as a heathen and a publican." and "He that believeth you believeth me...." It is not the Bible, but faith, that causes Catholics to believe all the Church teaches. We cannot let our guide be private interpretation of the Scripture.

Are You Interpreting the Bible Correctly?

The Bible says it will be hard for a rich man to enter Heaven, as hard as for a camel to pass through the eye of a needle. The eye of the needle is here to be understood to mean the small entrances leading into the ancient cities. Often merchants had to unload the camels to squeeze them through. To know the true meaning of the Bible is to know the meaning of the ancients, and for this we turn to the Church. Another example which may baffle some are the words of Christ while He was nailed to the cross. "My God, why hast Thou forsaken Me?" Some Protestants will claim that Jesus had lost touch with God the Father for a split second. But this is totally unwarranted. Yes, it does sound like a cry of despair and may make one wonder if Christ was divine. Those who wrote the Gospel knew that Christ was praying and these words are only the first verse of Psalm 22, which He was quoting as His death fulfilled the Scripture. Christ's suffering and death are set forth so vividly and yet were written years before.

> They tear holes in my hands and my feet and lay me in the dust of death. I can count every one of my bones. These people stare at me and gloat: they divide my clothing among them, they cast lots for my robe.

It is necessary to recall that Christ was the true God and true man. As man, Christ had the weakness and fear of our common manhood, which are notably expressed in the whole episode of the Passion, beginning with the Agony in the Garden. Here we see Christ asking the Father "to let this passion pass from me." We are also told that His apprehension of what lay before Him was the cause of His bloody sweat. So the text in Psalm 22 is simply another expression of the fear of dereliction coming from the soul of Christ.

I have just given two examples of Biblical misinterpretation. The Bible is filled with passages that can be misunderstood. The word of God becomes clear when it comes to us in the language of the writer, in his own time. The Holy Spirit dwells within the Church, leading it to all truths. Hence, if some passages of Scripture seem to say something contrary to the teachings of the Church, one will know that they have been misunderstood.

The Witness and Blood Transfusion

Another outstanding example of the meaning of the Bible
being misconstrued is by the Jehovah's Witnesses and their
strange teachings about blood. As is well known, the Witnesses
hold that blood transfusions are a violation of God's law. There
are even instances where they have permitted persons to die
rather than resort to this remedy to preserve life. Their idea
comes from the Old Testament: the eating of blood was forbidden
by many passages of the Mosaic Law. The reason for this appears
in Leviticus 17:11 and 12. "Since the life of a living body is in its
blood...no one among you, not even a resident alien, may partake
of blood." In other words, blood, like breath, was regarded as the
concrete embodiment of life, the gift of God and therefore a thing
sacred to God. Blood, according to the Law of Moses, was to be
used in certain sacred functions of Old Testament rituals, among
them the rite whereby atonement was made for sins through
various rituals of animal sacrifice. To this day, orthodox Jews do
not eat the meat that has not been drained of its blood. This is
one of the kosher laws.

Not even the most orthodox Jew believes that this law constitutes a prohibition against blood transfusion. In coming to such a
conclusion, the Witnesses have "out-rabbied" the Rabbis of past
ages. For this law against eating blood obviously had nothing to
do with human blood. I pity those devout Christians who believe
in the self-proclaimed prophet Pastor Russel of the Jehovah's
Witnesses and his predictions on the second coming of Christ in
1874 and his belief in pyramidology, finding reference to the
Gospel in the Great Pyramid, in such passages as Isaih 19, "It will
be a sign and a witness to the Lord of hosts in the land of Egypt...."
It's unbelievable, but people will accept anything that some
preachers say. Sects will come and go as did the Puritans, but the
Catholic Church will stand forever.

Still, there are many passages of the Bible that puzzle scholars.
Through the teachings of the Living Church they know at least
what these passages cannot be saying. Otherwise, God would

have abandoned that very institution which He brought into the world as the living pillar of truth; His Church.

Acknowledgement of the Books of the Bible in the New Testament

Before 200 A.D., most of the New Testament writings were acknowledged by the Universal Church as written by God Himself, through the hands of men, as were writings of the Old Testament. Before 400 A.D., all our New Testament writings had been carefully screened from other works that claimed divine origin, and were recognized as God's legacy to His Church for the instruction of the faithful in all ages. Proof of divine authorship in the New Testament is clear. First: these works had to propose the same truths of God as were being taught by His Church. Christ founded His Church as the living voice. Nothing that contradicted that living institution could have come from God. Second: these works had to be of Apostolic origin, either directly written by an Apostle or acknowledged as authoritative in Apostolic times. It was through the Twelve Apostles that Christ said He found His living Church. Third: these works made up the Bible that the Church used in the divine worship and instruction of the people throughout the world until Christ would come again in glory.

Therefore, the Bible could not betray His commission when used by the Church under the guidance of the Holy Spirit of truth. These writings were thus known as inspired by God. Through these three conditions, then, was established by the end of the fourth century the true writings of God after the time of Jesus.

The Old Testament

If you are aware of the content of the Old Testament used by Catholics and that used by other Christians, you know that there is a considerable difference. In Catholic Bibles, there are seven extra books: the book of Tobias, Judith, Wisdom, Sirach, Baruch, and One and Two Maccabees. There are also portions of Daniel and Esther to be found. It is important to see how this difference came about. The Church at the time of Jesus had gathered many of these writings, but at no point up to then had God said that this was enough. In fact, God continued the process of inspiration through the age of the Apostles.

When Christ came among men, there was yet another group of writings produced in the Old Testament Church, but not yet finally recognized. The widely circulated Greek editions intermingled with the books that had already been acknowledged.

When Christ founded His Church as the perfection of the Church of the Old Testament, this Greek translation with its extra books and parts of the other two became the official Bible of the Christian Church. As the true Church of God after the coming of Jesus, this Church had not only the duty but the right to decide on the inspiration of these books. During that period when the Church was investigating the divine origin of the New Testament writings, it was likewise looking into the origin of these books as of divine authorship. The result was that the Church admitted all of them to the canon of the scriptures, that is the list of inspired writings that God had ordained for His Church. These books were tested as true doctrine for the continual use in the worship and instruction of the Church.

The Reformers were Misled

For over a thousand years, these books were all accepted in and used by the Church. At the time of the Reformation, these books were rejected by most other Christian bodies. The Old Testament scriptures, as used among the Jewish people of Palestine, were considered the norm for content of the Old Testament. To be sure, the leaders of Judaism had determined that the scriptures were completed with their Bible and there could be no additions. But that decision was taken about 100 A.D., several generations after the coming of Christ, and at a period when the Christians were already recognizing the inspired scripture containing the sayings and deeds of Christ recorded after His ascension to Heaven. Without a true appreciation of the living Church, embodying in its own life the teachings of Jesus, the Reformers were misled into rejecting what had been acknowledged as inspired in the Universal Church for a thousand years. I also believe these so-called "Catholic books" were rejected by Protestants in order to conform to their doctrine of "justification by faith alone."

Some Protestants will lay claim that Jerome, one of the great theologians, condemned the Catholic editions of the Bible, the Apocrypha books. The truth of the matter is, he was the only one in the west to utter a protest against them. Jerome's personal feelings were that the books might not have been inspired by God. But he goes on to say, "Let them be read by the church for the edification of the people." Jerome did include the Greek additions to the Bible, not by way of condemning the seventy Hebrew writers, but simply that they might have been overlooked by the Jewish canonists. Jerome did accept them as divine authorship as they were declared at the Council of Trent. "Not so!" the Protestant religions declared. They accepted what the Jews of Palestine declared to be the complete Bible, not what the Christians accepted. Some will show the proof of their belief. The Hebrew historian Josephus did not include the Greek editions. But are these the same Jews who possessed the books of the prophets and did not understand them, and therefore did not recognize Christ even when He came? The list made up by Josephus is quite different from the list made up by the Great Origen or Melito, but they were Christians.

Why Do Catholics Accept the Greek Bible?

The Septaugint (Greek) version of the Bible was used by the Apostles who wrote the New Testament.

1. Christ and His Apostles admitted as inspired the writings of the Hebrew and Greek books of the Old Testament. There are about 350 citations from these books in the New Testament. Paul (2 Tim 3:15, 16) tells us that these books were regarded as inspired.

2. Christ and His Apostles admitted the books of the Greek Bible as inspired. These extra books are found in the Catholic Bible.

3. The foregoing is reinforced by the usages of the primitive Church. It used the Greek Bible and quoted from Greek books and vested them with the same authority as the Hebrew books. Thus, the Apostolic Fathers of the church quoted from them. Clements of Rome quotes from Ecclesiastes, Wisdom, and the detero Fragments from Daniel. Similarly, Hermis, Hyppolitus, Iranaeus, Tertullian, and Cyprian. If during this time, Justin and Melitus use only the Hebrew books, it is because they were arguing with Jews.

Verification of Use

1. Comparing the Catholic Bible with the New Testament: compare Heb 1:3 with Wisdom 7:26; Heb 11:34-35 with 2 Macc 6:18 or 7:42; Matt 27:39 with Wisdom 2:17-18. Compare also Ephis 6:13 to Wisdom 5:18-19; Rom 1:20 with Wisdom 13:15; Rom 9:21 and Wisdom 15:7; Matt 6:14 with Eccles 28:2. Read also Matt 11:28. It is reminiscent of the closing of Ecclesiastes.

2. At the time of Christ and His Apostles, the Greek Bible was very widespread. The Apostles quote from it quite often. It was widely read by Jews and Christians. If some of its contents were not viewed as inspired, the Apostles would have and must have advised the Christians of the fact. But they did not do so. Of the 350 quotations from the Old in the New Testament, about 300 are from the Greek (Catholic) Bible.

Why Protestants Reject the Catholic Bible

The main reason is their agreement with the Jewish rabbis, who agreed around 100 A.D. that their Bible was complete. Reasons given: (1) The Old Testament books had to harmonize with the law; (2) They had to be written within a time frame; (3) The language had to be Hebrew; and (4) The books had to be written within or near Palestine.

Catholics Attacks Continue
From the First to the Twenty-First Centuries

Imagine, if you can, that the Apostles could hear what others are still saying about their Church: "These Christians worship bread and the ring of the Bishops; they also worship pictures and idols. How foolish they are." Believe it or not, the Apostles did hear such ridiculous accusations from people who had no idea of our faith and Church. There are still those today who believe such nonsense. The fact is, Christians were martyred in the first and second centuries for worshipping and drinking blood and for sacrificing children. Catholics have been persecuted in every generation and country because of vicious lies. Even today, it seems to be the intention of some to ridicule Catholics. Catholics can spend a lifetime without ever hearing a word against another religion. They have no idea what is going on in other denominations. But, others in Protestant Churches never seem to end their attacks against Catholics. Personal inquiry is unusual, for they accept what their leaders say about us.

If you doubt how Catholics are judged by your religious neighbor, ask about them. Their information, such as magazines or pamphlets, are usually offensive against Catholics. You will be shocked by the literature the Baptists distribute to their followers: articles such as "Can Catholics Go to Heaven?" and "When Rome Speaks, Catholics Listen." Some preachers claim that Catholics are told not to read the Bible. Some will say Rome is more concerned with obedience and loyalty than with truth and Scripture. Their sermons display fear of the Catholic Church; it's obvious when one is trying so hard to prove another wrong. They feel insecure about themselves. Some even find interpretation of the Pope as the anti-Christ.

True Church of Christ

Most Christians feel they are in the true church. Why do Catholics feel this way? Because their Church will be forever, the one which has always had a visible head, the Bishop of Rome, the successor to the chair of Peter. She was founded by Christ Himself with the promise that "the gates of Hell shall not prevail against her." "She is the kingdom of Christ which shall never be destroyed." The Protestant religions came into the world 1,500 years too late to be called the Religion of the Church of Christ. The true Church, as both the Old and New Testaments give account, was to continue pure and holy in all her teachings and doctrines even to the end of time. Therefore, if the teachings of Christ were true, there could be no other need for the so-called Protestant Reformation.

The true Church of Christ shall be without error; "His Church shall be built upon a rock," like the house of the wise builder of whom He speaks (Matt 7:25) and the gates of Hell, meaning the power of Satan, shall never prevail against it. Therefore, the Church could not fall into superstition or make an error, no matter what is said against Her.

Protestants Give Their Reasons for Criticism

When reading about Protestant objections to the Catholic Church, we sometimes discover the source of information. It usually comes from ex-Catholics or turncoat priests. Also, we hear unwarranted Bible quotes. Some preachers claim that Catholics are void in their religion and stay only because of family tradition. Many Protestant Bible scholars teach that the Catholic Church is described in Rev 17-18, although they're not certain, but the description fits. Other Protestants claim Catholics do not accept Christ as the head of our Church, but accept the Pope in Rome. Many non-Catholics misconstrue the truth about us by leaving out the all-important words: Visible Head of the Catholic Church.

Christ's Church Is Infallible

Christ has made His promise to the teachers of the Church (John 16:17): "I will ask the Father and he will give you another Paraclete that He may abide with you forever. The Spirit of Truth." And He assures them that this Spirit of Truth "Will teach them all things." And in Chapter 16:13 He says, "Shall teach them all truths."

Look to Isaih 59:20-21, which states that after the coming of the Redeemer (His spirit and His words, that is), what is taught shall be forever maintained by His Church through all generations.

>   This is my covenant, with them, saith the lord;
>   My Spirit, that is in thee and my words that I
>   have put in thy mouth, shall not depart nor of
>   the mouth of they seed or they seed's seed, saith
>   the Lord from henceforth and forever.

Thus, the true Church must be always infallible in all matters relating to faith so that She cannot add to or subtract from what Christ has taught. The Church is called by Paul (I Tim 3:15): "The pillar and ground of truth." You can see the infallibility of the Church of Christ, Psalms 72:5-7; Ps 89:3, 4, 27-37; Isai 9:6-7; Isai 60:11-12, 25-26; Isai 62:6; Jer 31:36-37; Jer 33:14-21; Ezek 37:16; Eph 4:11-14; Eph 5:23-24; and I Tim 3:14-15.

How then can any religion consider itself to be the true religion unless it acknowledges the whole Scripture, both of the Old and New Testaments from the beginning to the end, which in so many places assures us that the Church of Christ should never go astray? As everyone knows, the Protestant religion pretends to be a "Reformation" of the Catholic Church. Evidently, according to Protestants, the Catholics have gone astray. The building of these reformed churches is founded upon the idea of men such as Martin Luther, who claimed that Catholics have been corrupted by errors. In his Homily, "Pearls of Idolatry," Part 3, Luther says:

>   Learned and unlearned; all ages, sects and de-
>   grees of men, women and children, have been
>   at once drawn in abominable idolatry, of all
>   other voices most detested by God and damna-
>   ble to man, and that for the space of eight
>   hundred hears and more.

How then can it be true that the building of these reformed Protestant Churches is founded upon the Scripture, which in so many places promises that Christ shall never be corrupted by errors in matters of faith, much less for hundreds of years over-whelmed with idolatry? So, this accusation must be false. Only the Catholic can feel he has total certainty in matters of faith. It is the security of the same Church founded by Christ with Apostolic Succession. Catholics also have the infallible certainty of their doctrines of faith, tradition, Scripture, and the Church. What other religion can have so pure the Word of God?

Perpetual Continuance of the Catholic Church

What proof do we have of this perpetual continuance of the true Church, from many plain texts of Scripture, in which it has been promised by God? "The gates of Hell shall not prevail against it." "And behold I am with you all days, even to the consumption of the world." In the Old Testament it also has been foretold: "And He shall continue with the sun and before the moon, throughout all generations." "In His days, (that is, after the coming of Christ) shall justice spring up, and abundance of peace, until the moon be taken away." "In the days of those kingdoms the God of Heaven will set up a kingdom (the Church, or kingdom of Christ) that shall never be destroyed; and itself shall stand forever." (Matt 16 and 18, Ps 71, and Daniel 2)

Christ's Church is Always One

There is also proof that Christ's Church upon earth is always one. From the Canticle of Canticles: "My dove, My undefiled, is but one—fair as the moon, bright as the sun, terrible as an army set in array." "Other sheep I have, which are not of this fold," (the Gentile) "them also I must bring, and they shall hear My voice, and there shall be one fold, and one shepherd." "There is one body and one spirit, as you are called in one hope of your calling; one Lord, one faith, one baptism." We have already seen that the Church is a kingdom which shall stand forever, and therefore must be one; for "every kingdom divided against itself shall be made desolate, and every city or house divided against itself shall not stand." (John 10, Eph 4, Matt 12)

Reliable Testimony

In 325 A.D. was held the first council of the church since the days of the Apostles. Bishops from all over the world gathered together. This first council was recorded by Eusebius, Church historian. He writes of this first council, "We have our books. But we also attach great importance to the handing down of Christ's teachings by word of mouth. For some twenty years, even the Gospel accounts were preserved in this way by the Apostles. Documents can be forged, but the oral testimony of reliable men willing to die for their convictions give real security. Nor are there as many links in this doctrinal transmission line as you may think. The point I am making, then, is that if we had no Scriptures, we would still have reliable traditions through three generations of trustworthy men: such as from John the Apostle, through Polycarp the martyr to Irenaeus, Bishop, author, and martyr.

One Church

It's been admitted on all sides by Protestants and Catholics that Christ established one church. The Catholic Church is not a new religion: it began with Christ. It is the religion that is attacked by most other religions. Only Catholics can be sure that their Church can be no other than that which had its beginning in Christ, and as He promised, was to stand forever. Whenever Christ speaks of His Church, it is always in the singular. Christ says, "Hear the Church," not hear the churches, "I have built My Church upon a rock," and not My Churches upon a rock.... Whenever Christ speaks, whether in figures or parables of His Church, He always conveys to the mind a "Oneness," a union, a unity, unless you are reading a Bible that has been altered.

Where is the Church now, and which is the Church that has existed this long? All history informs us that it is the Catholic Church. She only among all will bear testimony to this. Not just history, but all the monuments of antiquity will proclaim it. If Protestants can admit this fact, why are they not Catholic? One reason is that Protestants assert that the Catholic Church is corrupt and has fallen into error, and because of that, it was necessary to establish a new church, a new religion.

Then it would seem, what Protestants are saying is that Christ has deceived us and lied, or how could the Catholic Church, that had been once the true Church, not be the true Church now? If this is correct, as the Protestants would have us believe, then Jesus must be a joker, or imposter, and He has deceived us. Thus Christianity can only be a false religion.

Christ's Church Must Be of All Nations

To prove that Christ's Church must be of all nations, we find many texts of Scripture in which the true Church is always represented as a congregation spread through the world.

"In thy seed shall all nations of the earth be blessed." (Gen 22:18)

"Ask of Me, and I will give thee the Gentiles for thine inheritance, and the utmost parts of the earth for thy possession." (Ps 21:28)

"And all the ends of the earth shall remember, and shall be converted to the Lord, and all the kindreds of the Gentiles, that thou may be My salvation even to the farthest part of the earth." (Isai 54:1-3)

See also Mal 1:11, Isai 2:2, Mich 4:2, Dan 2:21.

The True Church

As you can see, the true Church has been promised to be pure and holy and one in both the Old and New Testaments. The true Church will continue pure and holy in her doctrines in all ages and nations, even to the end of time. Consequently, could the true Church ever be in the need of reformation? That which was of the old must still be so. It would be vain to seek for the true Church among any of the sects or pretenders of reformation, because they all build upon the wrong foundation, that is, upon the idea that the true Church has gone astray. The true Church must also be Apostolical, derived by a succession from the Apostles.

Catholics are Pre-Judged as Corruptionists

I would like to show some of the methods that anti-Catholics use to condemn our Church's teachings. Baptism will sometimes come under fire from those who say you must be immersed in water. Catholics accept the fact that Jesus and His Apostles did sometimes baptize this way, but it was not necessary. The sacrament would not be denied to any that believed. Were there not men in prison who were baptized without being immersed in water? Was there not a scarce supply of water in the desert where some received Baptism? Thus, sprinkling water became used when necessary with the words of the sacrament.

The Seventh Day Adventists affirm a verdict of corruption for the Catholic Church for worshipping on Sunday. According to them, this is not correct. But God commanded us to rest on the seventh day. The word "Sabbath" means "to rest". The Jewish Sabbath is Saturday, and the early Christians chose Sunday for their day of rest.

To stir up devotion, the Catholic Church will use ceremonies relating to God's honor, but not without objections. Therefore, I refer to Scripture for our actions. For example, Christ frequently used ceremonies such as curing the man who was deaf and dumb; and curing he who was born blind; and again in breathing upon His Apostles, when He gave them the Holy Spirit. (Mark 7, John 9, and 20).

Protestantism disagrees on thousands of points, but on one they all agree: Rome is false, and Catholicism is corrupt. It's the belief among non-Catholics that Christianity was very pure in the beginning, but that in the Middle Ages it became corrupt. Protestants simply say that everyone knows it. Every one of their books asserts it; they need no facts. Catholics rate sin at a fixed price, and they get absolution for sins. Catholics make images of their God. Protestants are so sure because their teachers say so. It is preached in their churches every Sunday. What authority do these persons have to prejudge, or even to teach? Their principles are private judgment. Principles of Protestants do not recognize a teaching body, authorized and infallible, to instruct them in religion.

There are some accusations to which we must confess and plead guilty. These were men making mistakes, within the Church, as individuals. In the Church there are good and bad. Scandals will happen, and we acknowledge them as we also grieve for them. We get very little credit from the prejudiced for showing others the scandals and evil ones among us. These things will and can happen, in spite of our teachings, as they happen in all churches.

God-Made and Man-Made Churches

If the Catholic Church has fallen into error, then the gates of Hell have prevailed against her; and if the gates of Hell have prevailed against her, then Christ has not kept His promise and He has deceived us.

> Lo, says He, I, Jesus, the Son of the living God,
> I, the Infinite Wisdom, the Eternal Truth, am
> with you all days, even until the end of the world.

We have just read where Christ has promised His Church, the Spirit of Truth, to abide with Her forever. If, then, the Holy Spirit, the Spirit of truth, teaches the Church all truths, and forever, there never has been and never can be one single error in the Church of God. There cannot be any limitation on time. Christ did not say, "Hear my Church for a thousand years," but "Until the end of time."

Paul said, "The Church is the ground and pillar of truth," and so if you take away the authority of the Church and God, you will induce all kinds of error and blasphemous doctrine. You can see that from Scripture and history the Catholic is the one true Church founded by God. This is not so with the Protestant Churches; it's an historical fact. All Protestant institutions were founded by men; history will show their founders and dates.

History tells us that in the year 1520, the first Protestant came into the world. Martin Luther, a Catholic priest, fell away from the Church by breaking his vows and marrying a nun. Luther, who was excommunicated, started his own Church. He was the first to rebel against the Universal Church. To his followers he said, take the Bible for your guide, and they did so. Soon Luther's followers were quarreling with him and each other, as they had their own views on the interpretation of the Bible. Thus, these new religions were to lay claim that the old religion of their forefathers had been mistaken. They were going to correct the false doctrines of fifteen hundred years.

Next came John Calvin from Geneva. He established the Presbyterian Church.

Another to protest was Henry VIII of England. King Henry wanted a new wife, as he lusted for a certain Maid of Honor. Henry put his request to the Pope to be allowed to marry her. This was foolish, for the Pope could not go against the will of God. Christ says: "If a man put away his wife and marrieth another he committeth adultery." Before long, Henry took a new wife anyway. Soon she was followed by a third, then a fourth, a fifth, and sixth. Here we have the founder of the Church of England who began his own religion to conform to his needs and, therefore, not the religion of God but of England.

After Episcopalianism came the Methodists, started by John Wesley. At first he was a member of the Episcopal Church; later he joined the Moravion Brethren, but not liking them, he started a religion of this own: the Methodist Church.

Of all these and other institutions created by man, the Catholic can at least feel comfort knowing their Church came from God.

Are Catholics Slaves of Rome?

Some Protestants claim that Catholics are to be condemned as slaves of Rome, that Catholics are misguided by their Church. Catholics "elect" to be guided by authority in their Spiritual life. The meaning of the word "faith" is the freedom to believe, and it is faith in our church and our decision to obey that which we believe. It must be understood that Church authority is not confused with the power to enforce the commands of the Church. It is only to make the commands. This authority is and has always been accepted by the Catholics with confidence in our free will, and it is done so voluntarily.

From the time we are born until the time we die, we are all guided by the string of authority. Papal authority is no exception for the Catholic. Just as there is authority in Heaven with the Angels, then are we not to accept Church authority on earth? By their faith, Catholics accept the whole of God's revelation as taught by tradition and the Bible.

Church Authority

Throughout the history of the Old Testament, it was the authority to teach from the patriarch and prophets, they, the authoritative voices of God, they that listened and obeyed, because they were obeying the Divine Will. There were penalties, even death, for those who did not believe. When the Old made way for the New, Jesus fulfilled the prophecy with the seal of His miracles, proving He was divine as well as human. Jesus (God) came down and lived among us. He did not change upon this system. Christ never at any time indicated not to accept what cannot be proved or that which is beyond imagination or is a mystery to the mind. Did God declare that His Apostles and teachers were to be different from those of before? Did He at any time substitute private judgment for those that He taught? To go even further, did the Apostles teach or even their disciples teach "private judgment"? The answer is no, of course not. He taught the reverse.

Jesus, commissioning His ambassadors, promised to be with them, by His power and grace, until the end of time. His representatives were to be teachers like Himself (with authority), and not as scribes, theorists, or guessers of truth. They were ambassadors with His authority speaking with His voice:

> As the Father has sent me, so I send you. Ye shall be my witness in Jerusalem, and in all Judea, and Samaria and even to the uttermost part of the earth. He that heareth you heareth me.

The Church Is the Teacher

The Son of God has come and gone, but left behind His mystical body (the church), which, as His representative, can not teach anything false although there are some who believe God has left the Bible and its interpretation an open question without any infallible teacher.

As is known from Scripture and history, the Church even in the days of the Apostles had disputes. History shows how one would accept or deny what others would accept or deny. Just as the Church was to settle what was inspired and what was not, it was also the interpreter of Scripture. the Church had to settle some questions and correct others. It was this Church authority begun by the Apostles which brought most Protestants to reject the teachings of the Universal Church. Most historians admit the church was in need of reforms, but not in matters of doctrine. The Middle Ages did bring much abuse to the poor. Remember, the Church and State were one. Reformation correctly meant revolution in Church history. The reformers were not only to reject that which the Church taught, but to toy with its doctrines and interpret the Scripture as they saw fit. Let me show by example what was always accepted from Scripture about Church authority but can be understood in a different way by the new churches.

A Different Interpretation by Protestants

After sixteen hundred years, we see a different interpretation by Protestants; an example is stated in two different ways in Matthew 16:16.

> And I say unto thee thou art Peter and upon this rock (meaning Himself, Jesus) I will build My Church.
> Thou art Peter a trivial little stone) and upon this (eternal boulder) rock (Christ Himself), I will build my church.

According to the Catholic interpretation in all ages, the simple reading of the text of Matthew makes it evident that Christ was addressing Peter. The significance in this term is a firm, immovable rock. The declaration of Jesus really should be rendered:

> And I say unto thee, thou art Rock and upon this
> Rock I will build My Church, and the gates of
> Hell shall not prevail against it.

Much of the force of Jesus' declaration is lost by the employment of the two terms in the Greek (*Petros* and *Petra*) that represent the original Aramaic. It is therefore evident that Christ employed but one term, and that there is an absolute identity between the term used as the surname of Simon and the term used for the foundation of the Church. The writer of the Greek simply gave to the term, when used as a surname of Simon, a masculine ending for the sake of grace of language, since both terms mean a rock. In a manner of speaking, it is unfortunate that we haven't an English proper name for Rock to conform to the Aramaic usage.

Keys (Power and Authority)

From Matthew 16:19, "I will give unto thee the keys of the kingdom of Heaven." Under the figure of keys, Christ ensured Peter as the chief authority of His Church. It is as when a king gives to one of his officers the keys to a city. He thereby declares that he makes him governor of that city. From this plain Scripture you can see the supremacy given to Peter and, consequently, like the Church, the authority will stand forever.

There are several Scripture passages which clearly indicate the word "keys," meaning power and authority. In Isaiah 22:22 or Rev 1:17, the words "binding" and "loosing" seem to be the terms taken from the Semitic language as used in the Jewish literature of the time. The words expressed wide authority, such as that of admitting persons or excluding them from the community, or admitting or excluding doctrines as authentic teachings. Consideration of this fact has led many impartial scholars to admit a real fullness of power for Peter to act as Christ's vicar. Authority can also be seen in Acts: "Appoint elders for them in every church." James governed the Church of Jerusalem in association with a body of elders. Thes 5:12 refers to persons who "are over you in the Lord."

Authority In Sacred Tradition

Irenaeus: The Apostles handed over "their teaching role" to the bishops.

Ambrose: Writes of the Pope, "The Vicar of Christ is love."

Augustine: Called the Catholic Church, "The City of God."

Jerome: Acknowledged the authority of the Pope.

> I think it my duty to consult the chair of Peter....My words are spoken to the successor of the fisherman, to the disciple of the cross. As I follow no leader save Christ, so I communicate with none but your blessedness, that is the chair of Peter. For this I know, is the rock on which the Church is built! This is the ark of Noah, and he who is not found in it shall perish when the flood prevails.

Protestants Deny Church Authority

Luther, Zwingle, Calvin and others claimed the same power and authority as the Church, that is, to be the judge and the interpreter of Scripture. Confusion on doctrinal subjects became contempt as they relied on individual interpretation. They taught others to decide for themselves the meaning of the Bible as long as these others agreed with them. But it was not to happen. Luther himself speaks of the "failure of this new doctrine, private interpretation:"

> This one will not hear of Baptism, that one denies the Sacraments, another puts a world between this and the last days! There are about as many sects and creeds as heads. No yokel is so rude but when he has dreams and fancies...himself inspired by the Holy Ghost and must be a prophet.

Authority in Heaven

The Lord's Prayer states: "Thy will be done as it is in Heaven."

It seems that God willed that there should be a chief among the Angels in Heaven. Scripture tells us in Daniel 10:13 that Michael is the chief Angel. If, then, we see authority in Heaven among the angels, what more can the body of Christ on earth be without authority? Who, then, can deny that it should be different on earth? God is God of Heaven and earth.

Chapter 3
Justification

Catholic and Protestant Opposition in Theology

The phrase, "Justification by faith alone," which many Protestants use, simply means to be justified by God. You can be saved by trusting (believing) in the grace of God revealed in Jesus Christ. To be "justified by God" means to be righteous before God, and to be regarded as righteous by Him. Those who believe in Justification feel that Christ had finished all that was necessary for our salvation. Christians have only to receive Him as their savior. "Believe on the Lord Jesus Christ and thou shalt be saved." Accordingly, there seems that nothing else is necessary; not even good works, charity, prayer, fasting, penance or even the fear of God's justice.

Martin Luther insisted that the Bible was the complete and infallible word of God. Still, he contradicts his own decision. First he removes the second book of Maccabees, and then ridicules the Epistle of James. The Apostle insisted on doing good works: "For even as the body without the spirit is dead, so also faith without works is dead."

Both Paul and James taught that in the Christian soul, faith and charity should go hand-in-hand producing deeds worthy of a Christian. By this, the soul of the sinner would be lifted to the state of grace. The gift of grace is a free gift of God, which must enter us as we obey the impulses of the Holy Spirit moving our hearts. Did Adam or Lucifer have faith, but lose sanctifying grace?

When Paul teaches that we are saved by faith with works of the law, he teaches that we are saved by a living faith, active through love. By the works of the Law he meant the works of the

Law of the Old Testament. Both the Laws of Moses, such as circumcision, and the Law of nature were necessary work performed to merit or effect justification. It may seem that an apparent contradiction of the two Apostles has occurred, but obviously James teaches that we are justified by works, not merely by faith alone.

In the James's Epistle addressed to all Christian Churches, he insists on the necessity of good works for the soul filled with active and living faith. James corrects the erroneous interpretation given in many places to the doctrine of Paul, in which false interpreters of Paul insist that charity is not necessary for salvation. Thus, we see the declaration of James:

> Be ye doers of the word, and not hearers only,
> deceiving your own selves. If then you fulfill the
> royal law, according to the Scriptures, thou shalt
> love thy neighbor as thyself, you do well. What
> shall it profit my brethren, if a man say he hath
> faith but hath not works?

Paul says in Philip 1:12: "Work out your salvation with fear and trembling."

Look at the words "work out" and explain to me how you can be saved by just saying, "I take Christ as my personal Savior." Paul also writes (Rom 6:23), "For the wages of sin is death."

According to Catholic teaching, faith is a prerequisite for achieving salvation. Protestant theology was in opposition to Catholic theology in that Protestants demanded other acts: fear of Divine justice, hope in God's mercy, hating sin, receiving Baptism. Faith must not be absent as also sorrow for sins. Forgiveness cannot be present without an inner feeling of sorrow.

> Acts 3:19: Repent, then, and turn to God, so that
> He will wipe away your sins.
> Luke 15:10: There shall be joy before the angels
> of God, upon one sinner doing penance.

Faith, Hope, and Charity

In Justification, people receive together the three virtues of Faith, Hope, and Charity and their remission of sins.

Rom 5:5: The charity of God is poured forth in our hearts by the Holy Spirit who is given to us.

Cor 13:8: Charity never falleth away.

From such passages, it is obvious that the two are inseparable: charity and sanctifying grace. These gifts are given to the recipient and are always infused when Justification takes place.

Faith as a certainty for Justification or sanctifying grace cannot be known without a special Divine revelation. The Council of Trent declared:

If one considers his own weakness and his defective disposition, he may well be fearful and anxious as to his state of grace....Nobody knows with the certainty of faith alone, that he has achieved the grace of God.

Scripture will bear witness:

I Cor 4:4: For I am not conscience to myself of anything. Yet am I not hereby justified.

II Pet 3:18: Grow in Grace.

Apoc 22:11: He that is just, let him be justified still.

Rom 2:6: Every man shall receive his own rewards according to his labor.

From the Sermon on the Mount, Jesus promises rich rewards to those who are persecuted for His sake (Matt 5:12): "Be glad and rejoice, for your reward is very great in Heaven."

From the writings of the early Church fathers we may recall the importance of doing good works. Chrysostom writes, "Seek faith, hope, and charity for they are greater than miracles." Augustine writes, "Without love, faith can indeed exist, but be of no avail." We also have the words of God Himself: "Unless you become as little children, you shall not enter into the kingdom of God."

Faith

Faith is the consequence of the "will to believe." Then, if you do not believe, it is your will at fault. You must struggle in prayer and constantly for the gift of grace to believe.

It is a mistake for anyone to lay down the conditions by which they will serve God! Do not be fooled; when you are saying you are pleasing God, when you are only pleasing yourself. Remember the prayer of Jesus, "Not My will but thine be done." Peter did not struggle in prayer about this temptation, causing him to deny his Master, for Whom he had protested he was ready to die.

From the words of Christ, we know that faith is necessary for salvation. I ask what kind of faith must I have to be saved? Will any faith do? No, not any faith will do. The Devil himself will be saved. As the Bible tells us, "The devils believe and tremble." When God reveals a truth and teaches us something, He wants us to believe, or his revelation would be an insult to God.

After showing the difficulties that Protestants and Catholics have when confronted with the topic of "Justification by faith alone," we've examined only one in many topics that separate Christians. How do we as Catholics know if we have been justified or predestined for Heaven? I would like to share with you the brief biography of Saint Clair of the Cross, and the signs of election. The following information was supplied by the Franciscan Sisters of Saint Elizebeth, Montefalco, Italy.

St. Clair of the Cross

Like so many other towns in Umbria, Montefalco is a small city set on a hill. It overlooks the valley of Spoleto, and some distance to the north, Assisi is visible. Here Clair Damiani was born about 1268, and as a little girl of six she was placed in the convent of St. Illuminata, where her sister Jane was superior. From the beginning, Little Clair observed the rule of the Third Order of St. Francis and added severe penance, keeping strict silence, taking only bread and water, and sleeping on the ground. About eight years later, Clair and the other sisters moved to a new convent, that of Santa Croce, which had been built for them on a nearby hill. During these years, they all followed the rule of the Third Order, but, in 1290, the Bishop of Spoleto substituted the rule of St. Augustine.

After the death of her sister in 1298, Clair distinguished herself by her spirit of prayer and penance and was, at about thirty years of age, chosen Superior. Not only did she carry out her duties as a religious and a superior in an exemplary manner, she also exerted an extraordinary influence on the outside world. She confuted heretics, converted sinners, reconciled families at odds with one another, made peace between neighboring, warring towns, drove out devils, foretold future events, healed the sick, and raised the dead. During the latter part of her life, she also received the gifts of ecstasy and supernatural knowledge.

It is related that our Lord, carrying His cross, appeared to her and said:

> I have been searching for a long time, daughter,
> to find a firm and solid place on which to plant
> My cross, and I have not found one more suit-
> able than your heart. You must receive it and
> allow it to take root.

Clair herself once told a sister in her convent: "If you seek the Cross of Christ, take my heart. There you will find the suffering Lord." There is good evidence that when her heart was opened after her death, the Cross and other instruments of the Passion were found within, embedded in fibrous tissue. For this reason she is also called St. Clair of the Cross. There pellets were also found in the gall of the Saint at the time of the extraction of her heart. These pellets were judged by theologians to be symbols of the Trinity as it was found that any one of them was as heavy as the other, and any one of them equaled the weight of all three together.

Clair died at the age of forty on August 17, 1308, and was buried in the chapel of Santa Croce Convent. Later, a church was built next to the chapel and dedicated to her. Here, her body, which has been preserved incorrupt in a most unusual manner, can still be seen; in fact, it seems to be that of a living person who is asleep. It is also claimed that the miracles of liquefaction and ebullition (bubbling up) of her blood have taken place. The cult which had been paid to her as Blessed from the time of her death was approved in 1624; and in 1881 Pope Leo XIII canonized her.

The miraculous preservation of the incorrupt body of St. Clair, her heart and the three pellets, can also still be seen in her shrine in the Church of the Holy cross in Montefalco, Italy.

The Signs of Election

(1) Consider what a consolation it must have been for St. Clair to have the Cross of Christ imprinted on her heart. Who of us would not rejoice at such a sign? Our Faith teaches us that no man, unless it has been divinely revealed to him, is certain of his salvation. But there are general signs from which we may confidently draw hope. If at times God revealed to certain souls that their salvation was assured, they were such who had long before borne these general signs of predestination which the Apostle designates when he says: "For whom He foreknew, He also predestined to be made conformable to the image of His Son."

True imitation of Christ, which consists in denying oneself and carrying the cross sent, is the first and surest sign of predestination. Is this sign discernable to you?

(2) Consider that other signs of predestination are sentiments of penance and mortification. Even sinners are not cut off from salvation, for "Christ Jesus came into the world to save sinners." But they can get there only on the road of penance. If a sinner has been sincerely converted and lives in the spirit of penance, that is, renounces the desires of the flesh and the dangerous pleasures of the world, he may hope to persevere on the road to justice, and assure his salvation. Of course, he cannot then indulge in the spirit of the majority of men; but this detachment will be a sign of his election, for

> broad is the way that leads to destruction, and
> many there are who go in by this way; but narrow

is the gate and straight is the way that leads to
life, and few there are that find it.

(3) Consider that the practice of good works is a third sign of predestination. For, although our salvation depends solely on the mercy of God, still in God's will no man is lost except through his own fault, and likewise no one is saved who has not merited it so far as he was able. Hence, St. Peter warns us: "Labor the more that by good works you may make sure your calling and election." These good works are above all the works of mercy and piety, and in a special way, also love for prayer and childlike veneration of the Blessed Virgin Mary. Rejoice if you can detect signs in yourself, and pray to God, Who wills that all should be saved, that His holy will may be fulfilled in you and everyone.

Chapter 4

The Teachings of the Twelve

(Proof Discovered after 1500 Years)

The Didache (before 100 A.D.) is the Greek name for the text entitled "The Teachings of the Lord to the Gentiles through the Twelve Apostles." It was discovered by Archbishop Bryennias in 1875, in a Greek monastery at Constantinople, and published by him in 1883. This document was written in the late First Century. Its author is anonymous. It is of extreme importance in that it confirms the many beliefs of the early Christians. We will gain from the knowledge of these long-lost pages, in details such as the life of the early Church. It is but another piece of evidence to assist Catholic tradition.

Before its discovery in 1875, we only knew of its existence in the early Church. For hundreds of years, theologians only had mention of it. Clement of Alexandria, who died about 217 A.D., quotes a passage which is found in this recovered text as being taken from the Scriptures.

There is one phrase, "If a man take from thee what is thine, ask it not again; for thou canst not," which has been supposed to be a reference to Luke 6:30. The coincidence is easily explained from the phrase quoted by supposing that the writer of the Didache and St. Luke both got this saying from the same sources of oral Apostolic tradition. It should be added that the author uses the name, "Christianos," which was invented at Antioch about 45 A.D. With these facts and others, some have given the Didache a date of some twenty years after the actual teachings of Christ. In writing about the Didache, I only wish to offer a fair contribution to modern criticism.

It seems evident there isn't a phrase in the whole text that a Catholic couldn't use today concerning faith and morals, such as "Commandments of the Church" as to fasting; almsgiving for "satisfaction of sins"; and the duty of confession before coming to public prayer (which involved Communion). All are startling testimonies to the Apostolic character of Catholic Teachings.

Eucharist

Concerning the Eucharist, give thanks thus: First, as to the chalice: We give thanks to Thee, our Father, for the holy Vine of David Thy servant, which Thou hast made known to us through Jesus Thy Child. Glory be to Thee forever.

And as to the bread that is broken: We give thanks to Thee, our Father, for the life and knowledge which Thou has made known to us through Jesus Thy Child. Glory be to Thee forever.... As this bread that is broken was scattered upon the mountains, and being gathered together from the ends of the earth into Thy kingdom. For Thine is the glory and power, through Jesus Christ, forever.... Let no one eat or drink of your Eucharist, except those who have been baptized into the name of the Lord. For it is concerning this the Lord hath said, give not that which is holy to dogs.

On the Lord's day of the Lord [gather] together and [break bread] and offer the [Eucharist], having first [confessed] your transgressions, that our sacrifice may be pure. Let everyone that hath a dispute with his friend not come together with you until they be reconciled, that your sacrifice be not profaned. For this is the word that was spoken by the Lord: In every place and time to offer to Me a pure sacrifice

> for I am a great King, said the Lord, and My
> Name is wonderful among the Gentiles.

From these quotations of the Didache, it will appear that the celebration of the Eucharist on the Lord's day was already styled as it continued to be long after in the Sub-Apostolic Fathers. Mention of Confession as a means and condition of forgiveness of sin so early in history is startling even to the Catholic. The discovery of this Antiquity is interesting for those who think that the Catholic Church was inventing these doctrines in the Dark Ages.

Baptism

> Baptize into the name of the Father, and the
> Son, and the Holy Ghost, in living water; but if
> thou has neither, pour water three times upon
> the head in the name of the Father, Son, and
> Holy Ghost.

We all know that immersion was common, but this text is perfectly explicit in asserting that it was not necessary. So, running water was preferred, as a symbol of the water of life, which in the Catacombs is always "flowing from the Rock." But this was only a preference, and any water, as the theologians have said, will do. The one thing essential is the water, the pouring on, and the Trinitarian formula. There is not a word which entitles anyone to say that the children of Christian parents went unbaptized. The doctrine of the Trinity is made sufficiently clear. "The Teachings of the Twelve" is as Catholic as anyone can desire.

Fasting and Prayer

> And for your fast, let them not be as the
> hypocrites: for they fast on Monday and Thurs-
> day: but ye shall fast on Wednesday and Friday.
>   And do not pray as the hypocrites, but as the
> Lord commands in the Gospel, thus shall ye
> pray: "Our Father, who art in Heaven, hallowed
> be Thy name, Thy Kingdom come, Thy will be

> done on earth as it is in Heaven: Give us this day
> our daily bread, and forgive us our debt as we
> forgive our debtors, and lead us not into temptation,
> but deliver us from evil. For Thine is the power and
> the glory, forever.

Surely, the most important point of the whole tract is the insistence, repeated once and again as a common idea, that this Eucharist was a sacrifice, a Sacrifice made in common and preeminently holy. The sacrifice was, indeed, ordained to replace for the new dispensation all the Temple offerings, and to be the true worship of the Lord in every place and time, and among all the nations that were to be gathered into the one fold.

In order for readers to appreciate for themselves the life of the early first century churches, the following are cited:

> Take heed that no one make thee to err out of
> this way of the Teaching, for he that doth is teaching
> thee away from God.

> For if thou art able to bear the whole yoke of the
> Lord, thou shalt be perfect; but if thou art not able,
> do what thou canst.

> And whoever saith in the spirit: Give me money
> or other things, ye shall not hearken to him: only if
> he bid you to give for others that are in want, let no
> man judge him.

Because the whole text would take more space than necessary to make my point, I offer only the noted citations. Some early churches thought The Teaching of the Twelve to be worthy enough to be used in church services, so, in a sense, it was accepted as inspired.

Chapter 5

Saint Peter

"Head of the Apostles"

In theology, there always seem to be two answers, the Catholic and the Protestant. I would like to give some of the reasons why the Catholic Church gives Peter and his successors so prominent a place in the Catholic Church.

According to Protestant teachings, the Pope is only a man, and not the successor to any Apostle; neither does he deserve that title. Their knowledgeable Bible teachers cannot find any evidence for Peter's acting as an authority figure within the New Testament church. Furthermore, they say, it was Paul who took the major role in the early church, not Peter.

Who Should be the Greater?

There were among the Apostles contentions as to who should be the leader, knowing the Master was soon to be taken from them. Their discussions took place before they received the Holy Spirit. It's true Christ had already pointed out Peter, but the Apostles at that time were still uneducated and unenlightened by the Holy Spirit. They were still mere men, suspicious of Peter's preference. They were jealous, yet sometimes mindful of the Master's exhortations about humility. In Luke 22:24-32, Christ's lesson was addressed to all of the Apostles. But, a special lesson was addressed to the chief among them: "He that is the greater...he that is the Leader." This clearly shows there was a "greater" and a "leader." Christ said, "Simon, Simon, behold Satan hath desired to have you, but I have prayed for thee, that thy faith fail not." Therefore, Peter's faith was not to fail, but to strengthen and keep together the rest of the Apostles. The danger from the temptation of fear was common to all, and all equally needed protection. Yet, special care was taken for Peter, he being their leader.

Peter Acts as a Judge
The Punishment of Ananias and Saphira

In Acts 4-5 we read of the punishment of Ananias and Saphira. The multitude of believers were to sell all they had and distribute it to the Apostles so it might be given to everyone according to their needs. Ananias and his wife were tempted and kept part of the money from the sale of their land. It was Peter who acted as the judge, though the other Apostles were present. He questioned and passed sentence upon them. The sentence was death, for lying to the Holy Spirit was violation of the law. The conduct of Peter in this matter, using his own initiative with others present, is a strong proof that Peter was chief or head of the Apostles, and that this position was acknowledged by them.

Peter's Shadow

All the Apostles, or at least many of them, took part in the working of signs and wonders, but special mention is made of Peter's miracles. Some of these miracles were worked as his shadow passed over the sick in their beds. Peter's superiority over the other Apostles seems to have been well known, for the people brought their sick and laid them in Peter's way, that his "shadow at the least might overshadow any of them, and they might be delivered from their infirmities." They knew his position and his power, and so sought him more than any other of the Apostles.

Peter's Sin

What was Peter's sin in denying Christ? Was it a sin against faith? I would say no, for Peter would not have followed Jesus into such a dangerous place. But he did lack the courage of a mortal man and was afraid. This fall of Peter is sometimes used as an argument against both the supremacy and the infallibility of Peter. Some reformers object, saying Peter had denied his Master three times, so then, how could he be head of the Church? I say do not confuse the issue of supremacy with sinlessness. To say that Peter was sinless or perfect is not part of Catholic teachings. And his sin, such as it was, does not concern his office as Chief Bishop. It was the private act of an individual, not an official act. To those who object to the sin of Peter we say, his act was not a falling away from faith but a falling from the outward profession of faith, and whatever his fault, it was not an official act; whereas Catholics hold true to Peter and his successors, the Bishop of Rome, who is infallible — not in private capacity, but only as head of the Church. He defined a doctrine concerning faith and morals to be held by the whole Church. Consider also that at the time of Peter's sin, he was not yet head of the Church and was, therefore, not yet infallible. Peter had only received the promise of the office, but was not yet appointed, because Christ Himself was still the visible head.

Peter is Marked with Honor

On Easter day, the Angel makes a distinct mention of Peter, as a mark of honor. At the tomb of Jesus, the angel speaks, "Tell his disciples and Peter." Even Paul, in relating the appearance of the risen Christ to the Apostles and others, said first, "that He was seen by Cephas (Peter)." This implies a manifestation of our Lord to Peter before He appeared to the others. It was fitting, then, that Christ first appeared to the Chief of the Apostles. In John 21, Peter is appointed to be shepherd over the flock of Christ, which is the whole Church. Even the most radical Protestants, who quote so well from the Bible, will know that the shepherd stood for authority. Peter's authority extends to all without exception. Apostles, Bishops, and all who come into the Church are committed to Peter's care. The Bishop is pastor over all in his diocese, Peter is pastor over the whole Church.

Peter Becomes the Chosen One

Chrysostom writes of Peter,

> He was the chosen one of the Apostles, the mouthpiece of the disciples, the leader of the

choir, and if anyone should say, "how then did James receive the title of Bishop of Jerusalem?" we can answer that Peter was appointed not only Bishop of Jerusalem, but of the whole world.

Again he writes "Why, then, did He shed his blood? That he might possess those sheep which He entrusted to Peter and to those after him?"

In Acts 3, the first miracle of Peter and John, if there were any of the Apostles higher than Peter, it would surely have been John. Yet, whenever these two men are associated in their works, it is Peter who is mentioned first. It is Peter who works the miracles. John is silent. Again, Peter takes up the words and speaks for himself and John: "See," Chrysostom states, "how John is on every occasion silent, which Peter defends him likewise."

In Acts 8:5-25, "They sent unto them Peter and John." This is a passage used by some Protestants to try to prove that Peter was not the chief among the Apostles, the sender being though greater than the one sent. To this I say, not so, for it is written, "God so loved the world as to send His Only Begotten Son," but the Son is Himself God, equal to the Father and the Holy Spirit. Again, Paul and Barnabas were sent by the church at Antioch. Paul's being sent by the Church officials at Antioch could in no way make him inferior to those persons. The act of sending was done with that person's consent and authority.

Peter as leader made his visits everywhere. James presided over the Church of Jerusalem, as others had taken their part in planting the Church in all nations. Peter was to be visiting all, for all were under his care. Peter was arrested, and "Prayer was made without ceasing." When James or Paul were arrested, there is no mention of prayer, though we cannot doubt there was no prayer for they were authority figures in the Church. Peter was more. He had the honor to be the leader, the visible head of the Church, as he or his successor were needed for the body of the Church.

Peter's name is always put in a place of honor; "Peter, James, and John." "Peter and John," "Simon and Peter standing up with the eleven." Sometimes he would be named last, in the case of the more important person named last, Peter is named last in, "I, indeed, am of Paul; and I, of Apollo; and I, Cephas (Peter); and I, of Christ...the rest of the Apostles, and the brethren of the Lord, and Cephas."

Peter, Supreme Authority

"Thou art Peter." This and the following text, of passages from those prove the primacy of Peter and His supreme authority under Jesus, over the Church. On first seeing Simon, even before Peter was called to be an Apostle, Christ said to him, "Thou art Simon. Thou shalt be called Peter." He again addresses him by the name he received at his circumcision, "Blessed art thou, Simon Bar-Jona" (Simon, son of John). Then Jesus makes the solemn change of names, "...and I say to thee that thou art Peter," (Cephas), meaning a rock. Why did Jesus call Simon a rock? He explains what He means: "And upon this rock (i.e. upon you, Simon) I will build My Church and the gates of hell shall not prevail against it."

Christ, in His address to Peter, is speaking of the spiritual Church made up of human beings, the society He came upon earth to begin, with true believers in Christ. He gained it by His Blood. To guarantee that His Church should last forever, He was going to raise it upon a firm, immovable foundation, which the devil, with all his power to rage, would never be able to overcome.

Christ Appoints Peter to Take His Place

Note the expression from Peter, "Lovest thou me more than these (the Apostles)." More love was asked from Peter because the charge committed to him was to be so great.

"Feed My lambs; feed My sheep." Under the figure of a shepherd feeding his sheep, Christ makes Peter the ruler of the Church, and gives him authority over all faithful. When Jesus spoke of Himself as the Good Shepherd, He said there was to be one fold and one Shepherd; this idea conveyed to us is connected with headship, authority, and submission to authority.

In the first and second exhortation of our Lord to Peter, "Feed My lambs...feed My sheep" the Greek word "boske" (and it must be remembered that John's Gospel was written originally in Greek) means simply to feed or to pasture, and with these words Peter exhorted the guidance and teaching of the faithful. But in the third exhortation, "feed My sheep" a different word is used, "poimine," which means "rule." This word is used again by Paul, when he tells the Bishops that they have been placed by the Holy Spirit "to rule the Church of God." And Peter exhorts the Bishops to "Feed the flock of God which is among you, taking care of it not by constraint, but willingly as of God." In these and other texts the Greek versions have the word "primainein" rule.

Therefore, it was Peter who was appointed to be Shepherd over all the rest, to guide and to rule the flock of Christ, which is the Church. Who are the lambs and sheeps of Christ? Surely, all who are believers in Him, all true followers of Christ. There is no exception made; Bishops, Pastors, and even the Apostles, are of the flock of Christ: all are committed to Peter's care.

"For Me and for thee" (Matt 17:23-26), is the payment of the tribute money. Christ had just declared that as the Son of God, He was free from the tribute paid to His Eternal Father; but being willing to pay, He associated Peter with Himself and by His power provided one coin to pay for both. So, you see the greatest honor and reward for Peter is faith when He connected Peter with Himself in the payment of the tribute.

Christ Prays for Peter

"I have prayed for thee." Satan's attack is directed against all: Christ prays for one, and by this prayer for one, Christ's prayer is unfailing. Now, what was Christ's prayer? "That faith fail not, and that, being once converted, confirm thy brethren." Therefore, Peter's faith was not to fail and he was to confirm, that is, to strengthen and keep together even the Apostles. This is a repetition of the promise already made to Peter, that he was to be the firm and immovable foundation on which the Church was to rest;

and there it is distinctly stated that even the pillars of the Church were to be kept firm by Peter. Leo writes of this passage:

In Peter, therefore, the fortitude of all is protected, and the help of Divine Grace is so ordered, that the firmness which Christ is given to Peter, is conferred through on the Apostles.

Christ had foreseen this fierce assault and had promised that neither this attempt to destroy the Church, nor future attempts, should succeed: "The gates of hell shall not prevail against it."

Was There a Division of Jurisdiction?

There are so many texts and passages from the Gospels and Acts that many arguments from the non-Catholic writers should be discussed. One such example is, "To me was committed the Gospel of the uncircumcision." From this, Protestants try to show there was a division of jurisdiction, Peter having authority over the Jews and Paul over the Gentiles. But if it was a division between Peter and Paul, what jurisdiction had the other Apostles? The commission to go and teach all nations was given to all the Apostles. We know Peter preached to Gentiles as well as Jews. He was the first to admit the Gentiles into the Church. Paul preached to the Jews as well as to Gentiles.

Peter's work lay chiefly among the Jews, and Paul's chiefly among the Gentiles. It was for this reason that one was called the "Minister of circumcision," and the other was called "The Apostle of the Gentiles." There is no proof for any separate and independent jurisdiction between Peter and Paul, for Peter had admitted the Gentiles into the Church and declared they were not bound to the Jewish Law of Circumcision.

It was not a legitimate point of doctrine, but of conduct. The events of the conduct at Antioch accordingly resulted in Peter's fault. As a dogmatic error, being injurious to the truth of the Gospel, Paul should have cautioned Peter against this fault. To all who know the Gospel, it is clear that by the voice of the Lord the care of the Church was committed to Peter. Doesn't it seem remarkable that Paul gives to Peter the same title that he gave to Christ, yet had power and authority over all?

The Church That Is In Babylon

Many Protestants claim that Peter's reference to Babylon in 1 Peter actually was Babylon. But to call Babylon "Rome" is a ridiculous assertion. Also, if Peter was in Rome, why did Paul not send greetings to Peter? Paul mentioned many people, but, amazingly, not Peter; and, of course, tradition (historical evidence) is rejected.

It was the established interpretation that the place meant was Rome. For we never hear of Peter's being in the East and the thing itself is improbable. Babylon was not the seat of a Christian community; the idea is only a reflection of prejudice of Catholic teachings and there is no trace of Peter's works or his presence in Babylon in any ancient records. All ancient authorities are unanimous that Peter spent the last years of his life in Rome. Babylon was the symbolical designation of Rome and must be understood as equivalent to Rome. Peter not only resided in Rome, but was the first Bishop of the Christian community. It was witnessed by numerous men of the Ancient Church.

From Tradition

We can learn from the early Church Fathers about Peter and how he was accepted with honor and authority:

Ambrose: "Christ is the rock, but yet He did not deny the grace of this name to His disciple."

Chrysotom: "The first of all and the chief, the mouth-piece of all the Apostles."

Cyprian: "There is one church founded by the Lord Christ upon Peter for the origin and purpose of unity."

Jerome: "Therefore is one chosen out of the twelve, that the occasion of schism be taken away."

Polycarp: "The greatest, most ancient and illustrious Church founded and constituted at Rome by the two most glorious Apostles, Peter and Paul."

Tertullian: "The Church of the Romans recounts that Clement was ordained by Peter."

Cyprian: (calls Rome) "The Chair of Peter and the ruling Church, hence the unity of the priesthood has its source."

Augustine: "Number up the Bishops from the very See of Peter, and in that order of Father's see who succeeded to whom. This is the rock the gates of hell overcome not."

Gregory the Great: "Who is ignorant that the holy Church is established on the firmness of the Chief of Apostles?"

If you question Christ's Church, listen to the words of Peter "to whom shall we go", for the answer is not private interpretation but the Catholic Church, founded by Christ Himself.

Chapter 6
The Blessed Mother

Mary

I would like to start again by giving the view of some Protestants concerning Mary and her role in the Church. "Yes, Catholics do worship Mary," by attributing the Immaculate Conception to her. Mary has no place in the salvation of a soul. Jesus Christ is our only intercessor, obviously. There is no need for Christ to have an assistant. We blaspheme when we give Mary or anyone else a mediatory role. The cult of Mary is a great fabrication against the Roman Church. Besides having no Scriptural proof, nothing is even mentioned in the early Church acknowledging Mary as the Mother of God, or that prayers should be offered to her. So say the Protestants.

Mary, the Blessed Mother

But the early fathers did speak of Mary, not only as the Mother of God, but as the "Second Eve". Irenaeus writes, about 180 A.D.:

Mary, by her obedience, became both to herself and to all mankind the cause of our salvation. The knot of Eve's disobedience was loosened by Mary's obedience. What the Virgin Eve bound by disbelief, the Virgin Mary unbound by faith. As by a virgin, the human race had been given over to death, so by a virgin it is saved.

Irenaeus knew Polycarp, a disciple of the Apostle John, and he testifies that the same preaching of the truth the Church received from the Apostles had come down to him in its purity.

Justin Martyr, who defended the faith by his writings, died a martyr less than fifty years after the death of John the Apostle.

He said, "Mary was descended in a direct line from King David." Her father's name was Joachim. The Jewish writers also gave him the name of Heli. The Arabic tradition of Palestine and the early commentators of the Koran call him Imran. His wife Anna, or Hanna, was of the tribe of Levi.

Mary's birthplace was the town of Nazareth in lower Galilee, also the home of Joseph. The child Mary was born on September 8 in the year of Rome 734, twenty years before the Christian era. In the Koran (Chapter 3), her mother is quoted:

> O, God, I have brought into the world a daughter,
> and I have named her Miriam (Mary). I place both
> her and her posterity under Thy protections,
> preserve them from the designs of Satan.

On her third birthday, Mary's parents took her from Nazareth to Jerusalem to fulfill their vow to consecrate her to the Temple of God. She was given to the priests of the temple, where she and other children by vow would be dedicated to the life of Nazarites. Her is where the life of Mary was spent from her third year upward. During the rule of Herod the Great, Mary was educated.

The "Proto Gospel of James" describes Mary as seated before a spindle of wool that was dyed purple. Besides this, Epiphanius says, Mary was skilled in embroidery and weaving fine linen and cloth of gold. As tradition informs us, her father died in her thirteenth year. She returned to Nazareth, and then her mother died. As Gregory of Nayssa relates, it was the tradition that her nearest relative should find her a protector and a husband among her own tribe, in accordance with the Mosaic Law. Even though she did not want to be married at that time, the orphan Mary did consent, as her relatives refused to let her return to the temple.

In the "Proto Gospel of James," Jerome, recalling the ancient tradition, tells us of the suitors. Among the unwed kinsmen of Mary's home, the descendants of David assembled. On the altar of the temple, they put a rod of almond tree by the suitors. The next morning, that which bore the name of Joseph was selected by Providence. Also according to the Proto Gospel, Joseph was an old man when he married Mary. Mary's occupation during the years of her public mission is verified by Tertullian and Celsus, an enemy of Christians. Both said that Mary supported herself by manual labor.

"Mother of God"

In the fifth century, Arianism denied the divinity of the Son of God and therefore refused Christ, the Incarnate Son, the title and quality of true God. Nestorius admitted the Son was God, but denied that the man Christ, born of the Virgin Mary, was in any sense the true God. These false teachings affirmed it was an error to say, "God was born of the Virgin Mary, suffered, rose from the tomb, and ascended into Heaven." The whole Nestorian controversy questioned the dogma, or doctrinal fact, as to whether Mary was and should be called "The Mother of God." On June 22, 431 A.D., a council was assembled at Ephesus, the city in which Mary spent the last years of her life. There, in the Cathedral Church, 160 bishops of the East and West met. Their session lasted until total agreement was received, condemning the teachings of the School of Nestorius. Thus, the Blessed Virgin Mary was declared to be the true "Mother of God," and her Son as God. While being human, Mary is the most highly honored of all created beings and He is the Creator.

The title, "Mother of God," confuses many Protestants. No Catholic believes that Mary came before God. She was never given the title "The Source of the Creator." Using the title, "Mother of God," we refer to the mystery of the Trinity and not to "God the Creator." Jesus had both divine and human natures united in one person. Of that human nature, Mary is the mother. The dogma of Mary proposed at the council of Ephesus 431 A.D., said that the same person who is the Son of God is also the Son of the Blessed Virgin.

We read in Luke 1:48, "For behold from henceforth, all generations shall call me blessed." These words are predictions of the honor which the Church in all ages should pay to the Blessed Mother. Let the Protestants examine whether they are in any way concerned in this prophecy.

The Manifestation of Christ

Mathetes, 130 A.D., disciple of the Apostles, writes to Diognetur:

> God Himself, who is almighty, the Creator of all things and invisible, has sent from Heaven, and placed among men, (Him who is) the truth, and the holy and incomprehensible Word. He did not, as one might have imagined, send any servant, or angel or ruler...but the Creator and Fashioner of all things.

Ignatius, 30-107 A.D., disciple of John, writes to the Trallians:

> Mary then did truly conceive a body which had God inhabiting it. And God the Word was truly born of the Virgin, having clothed Him with a body of like passions with our own. He who forms all men in the womb, was Himself really in the womb, and made for Him a body of the seed of the Virgin, but without any intercourse of men.

First Born

Protestants will sometimes take from Scripture (Matt 1:25), "Till she brought forth her first born son," to try to prove that Mary was the mother of more than one son. Jerome answers with Scripture example:

> The word of God defines first born as everything that openeth the womb. (See Num 18:15) Otherwise, if the title belongs to such only as having younger brothers, the priests cannot claim the firstling until their successors have been begotten. Wait until a second is born. I owe nothing to the priests. From Luke we know that every male that openeth the womb shall be called holy to the Lord and to offer a sacrifice. But insomuch as he who has no younger brothers is bound by the law of the first born, we gather that he is

called first born who opens the womb and has been preceded by none, not he whose birth is followed by that of a younger brother.

The Relationship of Jesus and James

The relationship of Jesus and James has often been a matter of dispute. Other children of Joseph and Mary are widely accepted in some Protestant Churches. Although there is the serious objection that while John was committed to Mary, in the letter of Jude he refers to himself as Jude, a servant of Jesus and brother of James. Can you see any claim to be the brother of Jesus, but not his servant? There is also the theory that Joseph was a widower and had other children before marrying Mary. If this is so, then Christ as a younger son of Joseph, could not have been regarded as the heir to the throne of David.

Jerome Against Helvidius

You have set on fire the temple of the Lord's body, you have defiled the sanctuary of the Holy Spirit from which you are determined to make a team of four brothers and a heap of sisters come forth.

I therefore come to the Gospel of John and there it is plainly written, "Philip findeth Nathaneal and said unto him, we have found him of whom Moses is the Law, and the prophets did write, Jesus of Nazareth, the son of Joseph." Now tell me, how is Jesus the son of Joseph when it is clear that He was begotten of the Holy Spirit?

Clearly, our Lord's brethren bore the name in the same way that Joseph was called his father. It was customary in Scripture for the same individual to bear different names. Peter is also called Simon and Cephas. Judas is called Thaddaeus. John's Gospel says, "But there were standing by the cross of Jesus his mother (and his mother's sister, Mary, wife of Clopas), and Mary

Magdalene." And according to the other Evangelist, this Mary was the mother of James the Less. Take note, also, the Lord's brother is also an Apostle, for Paul says, "But other of the Apostles saw I none, save James the Lord's brother." At this time, the other James was killed by Herod. So the only conclusion can be, James the Less was called brother to the Lord because of his relationship to Mary, the Mother of Jesus. James the Less, son of Mary, wife of Clopas, and again she is called wife of Alphaeus. To explain it there are two sisters named Mary. Jerome goes on to explain that in Scripture there are four kinds of brethren: by nature, race, kindred, and love. Jerome also states he followed the views of those before him.

Martin Luther sharply criticized many of the tributes paid to Mary. In Her honor, churches were built and feast days were instituted. She was also being glorified in many new hymns. Luther felt that divine honor was being given to Mary. Although the Church has made it clear Mary should be honored, the Father, Son, and Holy Spirit should be adored. Luther did hold the traditional belief in Mary, as the Mother of God, her perpetual virginity, her Immaculate conception, and making appeals for her intercession. But it did not last, for the doctrines of Luther ceased. The new Protestantism brought Mary down to the level of a model of morality. Still other new Protestant religions would bring their own ideas as to how or how not to show honor to the Mother of our Redeemer.

Immaculate Conception

By her Immaculate Conception, Mary shared in Christ's victory over sin: by her bodily assumption into Heaven, she shared in His victory over death. We must not forget the passage in Genesis which provides the basis for the belief of Catholics concerning Mary's place in the divine plan of our redemption and the privileges that were hers: "I will place enmities between thee and thy woman, between thy seed and her seed...." These things the Catholics believe are all truths revealed by God. His victory over death and sin, coupled with Mary's, can be found in the Old and New Testaments.

Mary's Part In God's Plan

Protestants usually ask, what does all this have to do with salvation? Did not Paul speak of Jesus as the one mediator between God and man? Did not Christ rebuke Mary on several occasions for meddling in His work?

Yes, Jesus was our sole Redeemer, the one Mediator in the divine plan. Nevertheless, Mary was also associated with the Mediator in the divine plan and played her part, an essential part, just as Eve had participated in the fall. Observe that the Angel sought her consent. In God's design, her consent was necessary. Mary, the Second Eve, by her consent cooperated in the redemption which Jesus won on the cross. Without diminishing in any way the gratitude which we owe our Heavenly Father, we acknowledge ourselves as wholly indebted to Jesus, our Savior. Our gratitude to our Lord is not diminished but increased by our gratitude to Mary. "So that by giving birth to the Living One, Mary became the Mother of all Living."

The Angel of God saluted her as "full of grace" and "blessed among woman." Never did a messenger from God address a human being in such language. There must have been a reason. No one knows the mysteries of God. Mary was a central figure in the early Church. She did not receive the same mission as the Apostles and disciples of Christ's Church. For this reason, no women in the Catholic Church have become priests.

The Assumption of Mary

By the Assumption of Mary, we mean that her body and soul were taken into Heaven, upon her death. The circumstances are unimportant. The fact that it took place is accepted as revealed by God. It is evident that the Assumption originated with the Apostles, for only through them have we a publicly revealed truth. Death of the body is a penalty of sin which mankind inherits with the sin itself. Mary did not inherit the sin of Adam and the penalties of sin. She was "full of grace."

In Scripture we find Mary is nearest to God as she is related to the Son by blood. Mary received the fullness of grace from the Father. She is the Spouse of the Holy Spirit. Who is in doubt that Mary, like Jesus, was without sin and, like her Son (Son of God), she also conquered death? If the body of Mary was not taken into Heaven, then where is it? All of the relics (bones) of the Apostles can be accounted for in Italy, Spain, and Turkey. It was characteristic of the early Church to enshrine the relics of the Apostles and Saints. Why was Mary, God's very Mother, neglected? Without Mary, who was without sin, there would be no God-man, Redeemer. Augustine writes of Mary in the fourth century:

> Whence, then do we know what excess of grace she was endowed in order to conquer sin in every regard, who merited to conceive and to bear Him of whom it is certain that He had no sin?

Images of Mary and the Saints

Questions often arise from separated Christians, why do Catholics worship pictures and statues of Mary and Saints? These same accusations were made by the reformers of the sixteenth century and answered, but Protestants seem to harp on the same old things, century after century. Sadly, the uninformed are never told the Catholic answers.

Catholics hold that statues and pictures of Christ and His Blessed Mother and of the Saints are to be retained and that due honor and veneration are to be given. By no means do Catholics worship images. No divine worship is given to a gold ring, or plaster, or stone, or a painting that resembles anyone in Heaven or on earth. It is the misunderstanding non-Catholics who make such foolish remarks, and whether they understand our faith or they pretend not to, it seems to be a good sermon against Catholics. Catholics are not taught to put their trust and confidence in images as the heathens did in their idols, as if there were a certain virtue, power, or divinity residing in them. Again, no, we do not pray to images, because as both our Church and common sense teach us, they can neither see, nor hear, nor help us.

What Catholics do is pray before an image, for example, of Christ upon the Cross, helping to enkindle devotion in our hearts towards Him that has loved us to the excess of laying down His life for the love of us. It is like looking at a picture of someone you love and miss and cannot be with. You may be talking to them, and they are not even there. Catholics call this relative honor, an honor which is given to a thing itself, but barely for the relation it has to something else; as when the Christians (from tradition) bow their heads to the name of Jesus, which is an image or remembrance of Jesus to the ear, as the crucifix is to the eye. So it's not worship buy honor, just as a Protestants will give honor to the name of Jesus, to the Bible, or their altar. The Jews gave honor to the ark, to the land on which they stood, as being holy ground.

To prove it is lawful to make or keep images of Mary and the Saints, we read what God Himself commanded to Moses: to make two cherubims (angels to guard Paradise) of gold, and place them at the two ends of the mercy seat, over the Ark of the Covenant, in the very sanctuary. God also commanded (Num 21:8) that a serpent of brass be made, for the healing of those who were bit by the fiery serpent, which serpent was an emblem of Christ (John 3:14). Catholics find no difficulties with Protestants when they paint the Holy Spirit under the figure of a dove, appearing that way when Christ was baptized or the painting of God the Father as an old man, because he appeared in that manner to Daniel.

Mary Appears at Fatima

Mary, the Mother of God, appeared to three children in Fatima, Portugal. This appearance of Mary is in no way a dogma of Catholic faith, although it has been expressed by many Popes and clergy as truly divine. I might add this evidence is not Scriptural, but historical, and, as usual, some Protestants feel it is only a hoax with a carnival atmosphere.

It was in May 1917, a memorable day in the religious history of Portugal. The Communists were in control of civil authority and were, at that time, imprisoning and torturing Catholic priests and nuns, as well as closing the churches. They did, in their state-run newspaper, report the happenings of the signs of Fatima with the headline, "Bewildering Happenings."

The Miracle Happens

As promised by the children, "Look to the sun," shouted Lucia, one of the three to whom Mary appeared. Thousands of amazed people fixed their eyes upon the sun, without pain or harm. It was reported that the sun was a whirling mass, its color white or silver, then turning to gold. Its shape changed to that of a flat plate, glowing with rich brilliance. The intense heat was sufficient to prove it was not the moon at which they were looking. It gave the appearance of a gigantic pinwheel. It happened three times, for about three minutes each time. After all this, horizontally moving and spinning, it moved and seemed to be falling from the sky, plunging in a zigzag fashion towards earth. The thousands of people were horrified at the spectacle; the sun was coming down, getting bigger and warmer. Imagine the fear; it must have seemed like the end of the world for believers, atheists, and skeptics. Yes, the communists were on hand to make sure the children did not pull a fake miracle. Just when it seemed to be the end of the world, the sun speedily took a zigzag path back into its position. Blinding sunlight returned, and the people quickly backed away with eyes blinking. What relief from their panic and what joy must have filled their hearts as they had just been witness to the greatest, long-awaited and much-publicized miracle.

Just as the Blessed Mother predicted, two of the children would be taken to Heaven soon. Francisco died in February 1919 from pneumonia. Jacinta died in February 1920 from pneumonia and tuberculosis. In 1951, the cause for their canonization had begun, and it was decided to exhume the remains of the two children. There was no problem identifying Jacinta, for her features are still preserved, but somewhat discolored. She could easily be recognized. Francisco's body completely disintegrated except for the skeleton. The third child, Lucia, still survives.

Was All This a Catholic Hoax?

Consider that, at the time, the Church was being persecuted and all religious gatherings were forbidden. Even though troops were dispatched, they could not stop almost a million people.

Here Are Some of the Facts

• Thousands of people saw the same thing happen. Was it mass hallucination or a supernatural event?

• There were thousands in the crowd whose purpose was to make sure the children did not pull a fake miracle; those who made no secret of their dislike of the Church.

• Many newspapers reported the dancing movement of the sun.

• In the official report on the event at Fatima, the mass dry cleaning was unexplainable. Before the sun danced, it was raining. The people were soaked and the ground was a pool of mud. Into this filth ran tens of thousands of people. When the sun-miracle was at its peak, everyone was wet and dirty, and when the sun resumed its place, the clothing of everyone was clean and dry. Even the most severe critic cannot explain these phenomena by natural causes.

• The Catholic Church at this time was fighting for survival in Portugal and did not want unfavorable publicity.

• Under the threat of death, the three children stuck to their story.

• The prediction that Jacinta and Francisco were soon going to die, while Lucia would remain alive came true.

• Finally, for the benefit of those who were not convinced, on June 26th, September 13th, and October 13th of 1927, Our Lady repeated the mystery with a tremendous beam of light, like a huge, heavenly searchlight with witnesses present and photographs taken for authentication.

Chapter 7
The Eucharist (Body of Christ)

To some Protestants, it is dreadful to believe in the Eucharist, while others say it is highly probable this sacrament is true. Sad to say, the Catholic is once again misunderstood and subjected to more erroneous attacks. To some Protestants, communion as described in the New Testament was only a meal of fellowship eaten as a memorial and a symbol of unity. The Bible will confirm that no repetition is needed of the Christ sacrifice. Also, the worship of a piece of bread, in the conviction that it is the Lord, constitutes idolatry according to Protestant interpretation of the Bible. Jesus was only speaking figuratively when He said, "This is my body... This is my blood." Read Acts 15:20, in which Christians are forbidden to drink blood. Catholics are only disguising Jesus as wine and bread. Furthermore, say detractors, no priest can miraculously change bread into the body of Christ, as it was decreed in the twelfth century.

First of all, Eucharist was decreed by Jesus, and God performs this miraculous change daily in His Church. Don't try to comprehend by your intellect what is possible with God. The Eucharist is Jesus personally present in the midst of us, seen in faith, received in substance, known by consciousness and adored. Study Jesus's answer to Peter. "Flesh and blood," is the knowledge which comes by sense, and reason "hath not revealed this unto thee, but my Father who is in Heaven." The Jews, who saw Jesus by senses, knew that He was a man. They wondered at His words, saying, "Whence hath this man letters, having never been learned?" Their senses carried them no further. Catholics believe by faith the Incarnate Word, and His revelation, and by His promise of presence and of power. Catholics understand that Jesus, by His

Divine power, is above nature, and faith alone is supreme. After the words of Jesus have been spoken, everything is as it is divinely declared to be. It is true we do not see the visible form of Jesus. In like manner, while He was upon earth His Godhead lay hidden, but His manhood was visible. Now, both lay hidden, and only His vesture is revealed.

Real Presence

To help you understand the doctrine of the Eucharist in relation to the real presence of Christ, you should know that the Miraculous intervention does not change the physical substance of bread and wine or the taste of bread and wine. We must conclude from Scripture that the ordinary does not happen to the Divine. No one can explain how Jesus entered through closed doors, or how Jesus walked on water. The Eucharist is accepted just as other Divine acts.

The Eucharist had been worshiped by Catholics long before the reformers started their new religions. Catholics have always believed in the presence of Jesus in the Eucharist, just as all Christians accept the soul attached to the body during life. The reformers replaced the body of Christ with a book. The Bible was the replacement for the presence of Jesus. Do they not feel robbed as they exclude Him in His tabernacle? Since their faith is not present in His words, then He is not present on their altar. According to His own words (John 6:53), the Eucharist is to be the source of life to all the faithful.

When Jesus spoke to the Apostles, they understood Him to promise He would return to them. "I will not leave you orphans, I will come to you." He came to them after He arose from the dead. It was in this sense that they understood His words. Before His Ascension, He said, "Behold, I am with you all days, even unto the consummation of the world." They understood Him to promise them a true and personal presence which would restore, for those in His Church, a nearness to all as God and Man. Therefore, it is as He said, "It is expedient for you that I go," for the coming of the Paraclete has brought with it the universal presence of

Jesus, not in one place but in all the churches abiding unto the end of the world.

Passover was a celebration by the Jews once a year as a memorial to remember their bondage in Egypt. The New Israel or the Christian similarly engage in a new covenant of redemption from the bondage of sin, by the suffering and death of Christ, by whose body and blood the covenant is ratified. The Eucharist, by the reference Sacrificial Meal, comes because the Church is conceived to be the temple of God and its living members are also a temple of God. It is sacrificial in the sense that it is the means of entering and sharing Christ's sacrifice. "Do this in remembrance of Me." In apostolic times, the word "Remembrance" does not justify the idea of today's meaning, not a mental picture of what is absent, but in the biblical word the meaning has the sense of recalling, of making what is past present again, so that it becomes operative by its effects, here and now. It is not that His sacrifice is repeated, but the offering is the recalling of His perfect obligation, so that the sacrifice is present by its effects.

In the writings of the early Church, there was a belief that the Eucharist was a sacrifice, being a pure offering of Malachi's predictions. It was sometimes the purpose of the early fathers to refute the erroneous rumors of those who wished to harm and accuse the Christians of illegal or pagan beliefs. It was their job to teach the truth and to convince others of the true Christian beliefs.

The Eucharist in the Prophecy of Malachi

Malachi 1:11, "And in every place there is a sacrifice, and is offered to my name a clean oblation." God is here proclaiming a new sacrifice, that is clean and pure. The sacrifice of the cross cannot be this, for it was offered in one place only. Reference to the Prophecy of Malachi to the Eucharist is found in the late first century writings, "The Teaching of the Twelve." The fact the Eucharist is an outward sacrificial gift is seen in Matthew 5:23, "If therefore thou offer thy gift at the altar, ..."

The Teaching of the Twelve
On the Lord's day gather together and break bread
and give thanks having first confessed your sins, that
our sacrifice may be pure.... For this is the word
that was spoken by the Lord: In every place and
time, offer to Me a pure sacrifice; for I am a great
King, saith the Lord.
The important point of the whole tract is that it repeats a
common idea, that the Eucharist was a sacrifice, the Sacrifice
ordained to replace, for the dispensation, all the temple offerings,
and to be a true worship of the Lord in every place and time.

Ignatius of Antioch (? - 107 A.D.)
Take care to partake of one Eucharist, for one is the
flesh of our Lord Jesus Christ, and one cup to unite
us with His blood. Let no man deceive himself; if a
man be not within the altar, he's denied of the bread
of God.

Justin Martyr (100 - 163 A.D.)
And this food is called the Eucharist, the flesh and
blood of Jesus who was made flesh.... The deacons
communicate each of those present and carry away
to the absent the blessed bread and wine and water.

Irenaeus (120 - 203 A.D.)
As the bread, which is produced from the earth,
receives the invocation of God, it is no longer
common bread.

Basil the Great (330 - 379 A.D.)
In Egypt, the laity for the most part had everyone
communion in their houses; and all those who dwell
alone in the desert, when there is no priest, keep the
communion at home and receive it at their own
hands.

Food of the Soul

The Jews had said, "How can this man give us his flesh to eat?" Peter also seemed to have been puzzled; but note the difference. The Jews understood not and went away. Peter also understood not, but yet he believed, as Catholics do today. In John's Gospel, Jesus said, "I am the bread of life." By the power of God given to His Apostles, we believe that the bread and wine offered at Mass has changed to the body and blood of Jesus; that which he gave us to be the food of our soul as we become united with Him.

In John we read, "The flesh profiteth nothing." But in Scripture, when the flesh and the Spirit are opposed to each other, the one means the mind of man unenlightened by grace; and the other, the Spirit is the mind so enlightened. Paul tells us, "The wisdom of the flesh is death; the wisdom of the spirit is life and peace." Therefore, the true meaning of this passage is that the doctrine of the Holy Eucharist just taught by our Lord is too strong a mystery to be received by man left to himself; it requires a strong act of faith with the help (grace) of the Holy Spirit.

We also learn from Paul that this sacrament was to continue in the Church until the Lord comes, until the day of judgment. I Corinthians 11:26: "For until the Lord comes, you proclaim His death whenever you eat this bread and drink from this cup."

Our Protestant friends are always asking, "What proof have you?" Read Matthew 26:26, Mark 14:22, Luke 22:19, and I Corinthians 11:25-26. "Take Ye, and eat; this is My body, which shall be delivered for you. This chalice is the New Testament in My blood" which are the words of Christ repeated in so many places. Without offering violence to the text, they mean a real change of the bread and wine into His body and blood. Also see I Corinthians 11:27-28: "Whosoever shall eat this bread or drink the cup of the Lord unworthily, shall be guilty of the body and blood of the Lord." Now how should a person be guilty of the body and blood of the Lord by receiving unworthily, if what he receives were only bread and wine, not the body of the Lord? Where should the crime be of not discerning the body of the Lord, if the body of the Lord were not there? In I Corinthians 10:16 we read,

> The chalice of benediction which we bless, is it not
> the communion of the blood of Christ? And the
> bread which we break, is it not the blessed
> Sacrament we really receive as the body of Christ?

No, Catholics do not believe the Apostles became cannibals at the Last Supper; they do not mention eating real skin or drinking real blood. We can only accept this mystery of the Eucharist and the words of Christ. He said the Holy Spirit will abide with his Church and He will abide with those who eat His flesh and drink His blood. "This is the bread that comes down from Heaven. Not as your fathers did eat manna and die. He that eateth this bread shall live forever."

We are commanded as we read in Luke 22:19 to receive the Sacrament in commemoration of Christ. And I Corinthians 11:26 lets us know what is to be the object of our remembrance when we receive, when Paul tells us, "You shall show (or show forth) the death of the Lord until He comes." But this remembrance is no opposite to the real presence of Christ's body and blood. On the contrary, what better remembrance than to receive, under the Sacramental veil, the same body and blood in which He suffered for us?

We do not blame Protestants for taking remembrance of Christ, but only for taking it as a bare remembrance, so as to exclude the reality of His body and blood, leaving out the substance where the words of Christ require that they acknowledge both. Catholics are blamed by some non-Catholics for worshiping bread. These foolish accusations are made against us, but Catholics do not dispute the power of God and accept His words, "This is my body."

Why Only the Body at Communion?

The Catholic Church professes that under either bread or wine, we receive Christ whole and His entire body, and that it's a true sacrament. To prove a point as to faith and reason, the living body of the Son of God cannot be whole without His blood, nor

His blood without His body, nor His body and blood without His soul and divinity. It's true He shed His blood for us in His passion, and His soul at death was parted from His body; but now He is risen from the dead, immortal and impassible and can shed His blood no more, nor die anymore. Therefore, whoever receives His body receives Christ Himself. There is no receiving Christ in parts. Yes, Christ does say in John 6:34, "Unless you eat the flesh of the son of Man, and drink His blood, you shall not have life." Yes, this is true, but according to the Catholic doctrine we do this, though we receive one kind alone, because in either kind, we receive both. Our adversaries, who receive neither one or the other, make this objection. But those Protestants who object to the real presence interpret the words of Christ differently. "Christ's words were not spoken of the sacrament, but of faith." And other Protestants claim, "The bread and wine are nothing more than symbols." So it can only be up to the individual to accept what his Church teaches. The Catholic accepts Christ's words as true. The Protestants feel that Christ did not really mean what He said.

Luther Attacks the Sacrament

Martin Luther, the hero and first preacher of the Protestant revolution, is witness to the first violent attacks on Catholic doctrines, mainly the Mass, which is the celebration of the Eucharist. It seems the Father of Protestants admits being taught by Satan. The latter is evident from his own words that appear in his book. (*The Mass and the Sacraments*, T. 7, Wit. fol 288). The abolishing of the Mass by the father of lies is no small part of his Reformation.

Chapter 8
Saints

The Invocation of the Saints

Although there is not much, if anything, in Holy Scripture that amounts to a direct authorization, we will see that Holy Scripture lays down principles from which the invocation of the Saints is legitimately inferred. If the Protestant doctrine of the all-sufficiency of Scripture were true, the absence of direct scriptural injunction to invoke the Saints would tell against it. It will give proof to show why the Catholic Church has accepted this belief for twenty-one centuries.

Take note that Catholics do not worship the Angels and Saints as God. We are taught that an honor is due the Angels and Saints. They offer prayers to God for us and confirm that their intercession is good. These faithful servants and messengers, having highly honored God, are now highly honored by Him, as He has promised (I Sam 2:30) "Them that glorify Me I will glorify." (Rom 13:7) "Honor to whom honor is due."

Protestants' Objections to Saints

Protestants' main objections are found in the words of Paul (Tim 2:5) "For there is one Mediator between God and man, the man Christ Jesus." We know there is conclusive condemnation of our prayers to the Saints. You will see, as Peter has warned, the words of the Bible can be misunderstood. First, take the example of the command forbidding us to be called Rabbi (Master): "For one is your Master even Christ; and call no man your Father upon earth; for He is your Father which is in Heaven." And yet we do apply these names to others besides God. It is understood that which is forbidden is not directed against bare words, but against a certain meaning of them. No one else can be Lord and Master and Father in the full sense in which God is our Lord, our Master, and our Father. And so, in like manner, no one can be our mediator in the full sense in which our Lord is such; and yet others may be our mediator in a lesser sense, as indeed, Moses is called in Scripture itself. (Gal 3:19) Protestants, who take scandal at our prayers to Saints, on the grounds that they set up other mediators by the side of Christ, should in consistency take a similar scandal at their own prayers for each other.

Other objections that are brought up are that the Saints could not know of so many prayers, or be able to grant so many requests. But this is easily set aside when we remember first that the power we ascribe to the Saints is that of intercession only, not of direct help. We do not doubt the power of God in giving the ability to know our requests to the Saints. It would seem their knowledge of our requests would surely be possessed, since they enjoy the Beatific Vision, as do the Angels. In Luke 15:15 we read "There shall be joy before the angels of God, upon one sinner doing penance." If there is a knowledge of repentance, what reason can we have to doubt their knowledge of our petitions also?

We do not deny ourselves the right to approach God through Christ, no matter how sinful we are. But, we do well to take with us the prayer and intercession of a Saint. Your defense dictates that Protestants might be correct if Catholics asked for the prayers of Saints in the same manner as asking the prayers of others on earth. But, who could think of going down on his knees to a brother on earth, singing and burning incense before him, when wishing to obtain his charity in prayer?

It is true there is a difference between our treatment of Saints and our brothers on earth. This veneration of Saints is rational. It has been shown that it is in accordance with nature to venerate the Crucifix because of its relation to Him whom it represents. In the same manner, the Saints, through their participation in His gifts and glory, make us revere them as the holders of these gifts. We revere them in a religious manner though, of course, in a way widely different from a religious veneration or Supreme worship, which we pay only to God Himself. Would you not show reverence and bow if you were to be in the presence of an Angel or Saint from Heaven?

To Prove the Saints Pray for Us

From Zacharias, we know an angel was praying for Jerusalem and the cities of Judah. From Apocalypse 5:8 "The smoke of the incense of the prayers of the Saints ascended up before God from the hand of the Angel." From this text, it is evident that both the Saints and Angels offer to God the prayers of the Saints, that is, of the faithful upon earth.

Remember, also, the doctrine of the Apostles (I Cor 13:8) that it is the property of the virtue of charity not to be lost in Heaven. How, then, can the Saints in Heaven, having so perfect a charity for us, not pray for us, since the first thing that charity prompts a person to do is to seek to assist those he loves? We can find in Luke 16:27-28 the rich glutton in Hell petitioning in favor of his five brethren here upon earth. Who are we to believe that the Saints in Heaven do not intercede for the brethren here?

See, also, Apocalypse 6:10 wherein the soul of the Martyrs pray for justice against their persecutors who had them put to death. How much more do they pray for mercy for the faithful children of the Church? Christ tells us (Luke 16:9) "Make to yourselves friends of the mammon of iniquity; that is, when you shall fail, they may receive you into everlasting dwellings." From this text, He gives us to understand that the servants of God, whom we have helped by our alms, help and assist us to enter into that same everlasting Kingdom after they themselves have risen to Heaven.

Paul, in almost all his epistles, desires that the faithful pray for him. Now, if it's acceptable to God and good and profitable to ourselves to seek the prayers and intercession of God's servants here on earth, then I would think it must be more so to seek the intercession of the Saints in Heaven since both their charity for us and their intercession with God are much greater now than when they were here upon earth.

We must remember when the Gospels or Acts speak of the Saints in Heaven they are equal in knowledge to the Angels. Christ tells us (Luke 20:35) "They are equal to the Angels." In Matthew 18:10, Christ said, "See that ye scandalize not one of these little ones: for their angels see the face of My Father Who is in Heaven." In other words, these children have powerful Angels to intercede for them in Heaven. The text talks of intercession for children, but we cannot suppose that if Angels intercede at all, they are restricted to children only. So, it seems obvious that if God can desire that the Angels pray for men on earth and can be moved by their prayers, what possible ground could He have for denying a like privilege to the Saints? It seems also that they are bound to us by a more common nature in every respect.

Catholics in their Creed profess the Communion of Saints, and Paul tells us (Heb 12:22) that we have a fellowship with the Saints in Heaven. "You are come to Mount Sion...to the company of many thousands of Angels and to the spirits of the just made perfect, and to Jesus the Mediator." Paul is saying we are all members of the same body under the same Head, which is Christ. Eph 2:19 tells us, also, that we are fellow citizens with the Saints (the just made perfect). I Corinthians 12:25-26: "And so there is no division in the body, but all its different parts have the same concern for one another."

Tradition

Our earliest theological writings for the canonization of a Saint come from Origen (185-251 A.D.), Christian Philosopher, scholar, and teacher, and one of the greatest thinkers of all time. Origen writes of those who have died and are in Heaven:

> Their virtue of love and charity are brought to
> fulfillment, as also is love. If the Christian virtue
> of love and charity towards others exist while on
> earth, then how much so it will be after death.

In the fourth century all the great Fathers of the Church agreed to the universal belief received through tradition. Thus, our own St. Chrysotom had a sermon about St. Berenice and St. Prosdoce, two martyrs, in which he says:

> Not only on this their festival, but also at other times, let us approach them to pray to them, invite them to be our patrons. They appeal to God with great confidence, not only whilst alive, but even more after death....For now they bear the marks (stigmata) of Christ, and whilst they display these, there is nothing they cannot persuade our Heavenly King to do.

St. Gregory of Nyssa, in his Homily on St. Theadore, prays to this martyr, and says to him

> If there be need of greater importunity, assemble...thy brother martyrs and implore with all. Remind Peter: arouse Paul: too the theologian and beloved disciples; that they have a care for the Churches they established.

St. Ambrose writes

> Angels are to be besought for us, who were given to us as guardians: martyrs are to be besought, whose patronage we seem to claim for ourselves by the pledge of the body....Let us not be ashamed to employ them as intercessors for our infirmity of the body even when they overcame.

St. Jerome prays to St. Paula, saying

> Farewell, Paula, help with thy prayers the extreme old age of the worshipper. Faith and good works join thee with Christ. Being in His presence thou wilt more easily obtain what thou askest.

St. Augustine, on the love of the dead, says that he can see no purpose in burying others near the shrine of the Saints, save while the living "remember them to the same Saints as do their patrons."

These five Fathers were the foremost of the fourth century when the persecution was over and the Church first began to develop a copious literature. Their language is distinct in expressing their inherited doctrine and not their own opinions.

The Church is Infallible

When the Catholic Church finally pronounces solemnly that a person is a Saint, it relies not just on human prudence. It has clear evidence at hand in the form of miracles worked by God through the intercession of the prospective Saint. That is the seal of the Divine approval on the sanctity of the person investigated.

Christ said to His Church, "Behold, I am with you all days, even unto the consummation of the world." This is a promise of special Divine help for the Church. Because of that promise, the Catholic Church canonizes a Saint who is infallible; it cannot make an error or cannot lead the whole Church astray.

St. Theresa and St. Antony

St. Theresa and St. Antony are two of the most popular Saints whom Catholics have chosen to adopt for their special patrons of intercession. Briefly, I would like to show why.

St. Theresa of Lisieux

St. Theresa's case is a bit extraordinary. No Saint in the Catholic Church in modern times has ever been conceded the title in so rapid a fashion. Only twenty-eight years elapsed between her death and the final declaration of her sainthood. With many of the Saints, hundreds of years have gone by before the Church felt ready to make a decision.

At the age of fifteen, Theresa entered the convent, and after the period of trial, was allowed to make vows binding herself perpetually to the way of life of the Carmelites. That was in 1890. The rule of the order was strict; fasting and long prayer were basic to the nun's daily life. Sister Theresa of the Child Jesus, as she was called, never left the convent. She died in 1897, when she was less than twenty-five years old.

The first step in investigation was a local examination directed by the Bishop. The court then proceeded to assemble evidence to prove that Theresa had a reputation for sanctity. All her letters and writings were collected and examined.

Nine of the nuns still living who knew her were questioned, and twenty-nine others were cited. Letters from her convent were also collected from those who claimed miracles through her intercession. The official job of one member of the court was to find reason why Theresa was not a holy person, or to prove these claims were only public opinion. The whole body of information was collected and sent to Rome.

In Rome the matter was taken in hand by a Cardinal who once more summoned an advisory board in writing and submitted to a board of Cardinals who voted on the matter without any objections. The decision was then brought to the attention of the Pope, who himself investigated the process thus far and authorized the Cardinals to begin the official hearings on the case. A new judicial process was then begun. All in all, ninety-one sessions were held.

Next came the examination of miracles. Of the vast number so reported, two were selected for examination. They needed something scientifically unexplainable. Charles Ann, a young man, was taken down by a serious case of pulmonary tuberculosis. Sister Louise was the victim of a severe gastric ulcer condition. Both recovered instantaneously and completely after asking for the prayers of Theresa.

These two reported cures were examined with all the scientific accuracy possible, and the nature of the rapid recovery was confirmed. In the cases in question, it was found that no medical treatment had been employed which could have affected the outcome. Five years elapsed between the cures in 1917 and the final decision in 1923. Two new miracles again were tested and proved. The process outlined in the case of St. Theresa may seem complicated and tedious, but this is the process taken. On May 17, 1925, Pope Pius XI solemnly declared Sister Theresa of the Child Jesus, known as the "Little Flower," to be a Saint of the Catholic Church.

St. Antony

St. Antony of Padua was not quite the person we would expect God to choose to manifest His power to the world, but God had called Antony to be the special wonder worker of his Order of Friars. Some Protestants declare that miracles ceased with the Apostolic Age. But those who knew St. Antony knew of his gift in its fullness in the form of inspired preaching and predictions. For the number of miraculous events, both great and trivial, many volumes would hardly find space; the power of nature seemed to wait upon, and to be altered at, his will. So strong was his protest against all false teachings that he was known as "The hammer of heretics." Some heretics heard of the Saint with awe, and under stress of his miracles, amended the errors of their ways. There were others who were less easily converted and attempted to poison his food but here also the sign of the Cross made a shower of the promise of our Lord: "If they shall drink any deadly thing, it shall not hurt them."

Antony opposed Eccelin, known as the tyrant of Padua, for his atrocities. After a massacre at Verona, the Saint approached him thus: "How long cruel tyrant wilt thou shed blood? Knowest not the vengeance of God is ready, and will surely smite, unless thou doest penance." So astonished was Eccelin that he cast himself at the Saint's feet in submission and confession. St. Antony, it seems, had a calling from Heaven to oppose Brother Elias, the successor of St. Francis, who encouraged a dangerous laxity. Because of this opposition, he laid down his office and retired to the strictest solitude he could find. He retired to the desert, but not for long. He grew weak and knew by revelation that the time was near for him to die. At the age of thirty-six he died, ten years a Franciscan. On June 15, 1231, St. Antony became the special helper of those who lost objects of value.

The process of canonization was begun at once because of the many miracles at Antony's tomb. Thirty-two years after his death, Antony's sacred relics were translated to a magnificent church still standing, which the inhabitants of Padua had built in his honor. His body had fallen into the customary decay which awaits our frail human flesh. The tongue alone remained incorrupt, red as in life; this according to Bonaventure, then General of the Franciscans, who assisted at the translation. Taking the holy relic in his hands, he said

> Blessed tongue who didst always praise God,
> who didst work so well that others might praise
> Him, now your merits are plain to all the world,
> and you received the recompense of Him Who
> created you for so glorious a work.

Relics

A relic is the body or a part of the body of a Saint as well as anything that belongs to the Saint. Do not foolishly believe that the miracles which occur, such as an instantaneous cure of an incurable disease, are the action of these relics. The practice of relics has come down to us from the first generations of Christians. Augustine writes, "Which God, whose truth sanctity itself would never have affected this honor paid to the precious remnants of His servants if they were not agreeable to Him."

The abuse of relics was a contributing cause of the Protestant revolts in the Medieval Ages. There was selling of relics as well as the circulation of false relics in which people died. Even towns and villages were resentful of each other for claiming to have faith in such physical objects, and in this I agree. It is through faith in God, with the help of the prayers of the Saint, that we receive His gifts. But, let us remember these Saints with our souvenirs and statues as we do with the memorials of George Washington. Are we not the better off if we are thinking of Christ and His servants with the aid of relics, which help us to be reminded of the honor due to God?

Jerome Defends the Use of Relics
Jerome Against Vigilantus A.D. 406

Although it is written concerning them,

> They follow the lamb, whither soever he goeth,
> if the lamb is present everywhere, the same must
> be believed by those who are with the Lamb.

And While the devil and the demons wander through the whole world...are martyrs after the shedding of their blood, to be kept out of sight.

Does the Bishop of Rome do wrong when he offers sacrifice to the Lord over the venerable bones of the dead men Peter and Paul, as we should say, but according to you a worthless bit of dust, and judges their tombs worthy to be Christ's altars? And not only is the Bishop of one city in error but the Bishops of the world....For in maintaining that the relics of the martyrs are to be trodden under foot, you forbid the shedding of their blood as being of no honor....How is it that poor, worthless dust and ashes are associated with this wondrous power of signs and miracles?

Jerome to Riparius A.D. 401

If the relics of the martyrs are not worthy of honor, how come we read, "Precious in the sight of the Lord is the death of His Saints?" If dead men's bones defile those that touch them, how come the dead Elisha raised another man also dead, and that life to the latter, from the body of the prophet, according to Vigilantus, must have been unclean? In that case every encampment of the host of Israel and the people of God was unclean; for they carried their unclean ashes into the holy land.

Once more, I ask, are the relics of the Martyrs unclean? If so, why did the Apostles allow themselves to wade in that funeral procession before the body, the unclean body of Stephen? Why did they make great lament over him, that their grief might be turned into our joy?

Still we honor the relics of the martyrs, that we adore Him whose martyrs they are. We honor the servants that their honor may be reflected upon their Lord Who Himself says, "He that receiveth you, receiveth me."

Chapter 9

Purgatory

Heaven or Hell, and No Purgatory

First, understand that the Protestant religions accept only Scripture as a bonafide record of God's revealed truths. Consider, too, that the Catholic Bible is different from the Protestant Bible. Your Bible, say the Protestants, contains the Maccabees as a record of the false practice which the Jews of the second century B.C. undertook. It plainly contradicts Scripture, which we shall prove. (Heb 9:10) "Having obtained eternal redemption for us...for by one offering he hath perfected forever them that are sanctified." Jesus Christ has done it all for us; there is nothing else to be added or done by man for those who are repentant and believing.

Prayers for the Dead

The Catholic Church teaches that Purgatory is a temporal punishment after death for venial sins and that the offering of prayer and Mass will help and aid those souls waiting, but unworthy of the sight and company of God. As to where this place is and the amount of the torment these souls must suffer, the Catholic Church has decided nothing. There are two reasons why Christians would go to Purgatory: (1) The person is formerly guilty of a greater sin and has not made full satisfaction for this sin or sins in the Divine justice of God; (2) Christians die guilty of lesser sins, which we call "venial" and haven't had time to repent. Catholics feel that as our soul departs this life and we haven't had a chance to confess our venial sins, we accept what the Church always taught, which is that we will not be condemned to the eternal torment of Hell. Does it make sense that these sins, which are small and which even God's best servants are more or less liable for, would deserve eternal punishment? Nor can the souls go straight to Heaven as the Scripture assures us (Apoc 21:27): "There shall not enter into it anything defiled." This, then, Christ assures: We are to render an account of even the smallest of sins against Him. Catholics base their belief in Purgatory on Scripture and sacred tradition and reasoning.

Scripture

Scripture in many places assures us that "God will render to every man according to his works" (Ps 62:12; Matt 16:27; Apoc 22:12). Now, this would not be true if there were no such thing as Purgatory, for how could God render to everyone according to his works if such a place did not exist? If someone should die with the least sin and not have time to blot it out by repentance, would he nevertheless go straight to Heaven? No, this would not be true if there were no such place as Purgatory. Every sin, no matter how small, defiles the soul. Hence, Christ assures us that we will be accountable for every idle word. (Matt 12:6) "Whosoever speaks against the Holy Spirit, it shall not be forgiven him, neither in this world or in the world to come." The last words clearly are to be understood. Sins that are not forgiven in this world may be forgiven in the world that is to come. Otherwise, why did Christ make any mention of forgiveness in the world to come? There must be a Purgatory; for in Hell there is no forgiveness, and in Heaven no sin. (I Cor 3:13-15)

> Every man's work shall be manifest, for the day of the Lord shall declare it, because it shall be revealed in fire; and the fire shall try every man's work of what sort it is. If any man's work abide which he hath built hereupon (that is, the foundation which is Jesus Christ) he shall receive a reward. If any man's work burn, he shall suffer loss; but he himself be saved, yet so by fire."

From this text, it appears that, with faith in the practice of their lives, they have stuck to the foundation, which is Christ Jesus, so as not to forfeit His grace by mortal sin, though they have otherwise been guilty of grater imperfections by building wood, hay, and stubble (I Cor 5:12) upon this foundation. It appears, I say, that according to the Apostles, man must pass through a fiery trial at the time that every man's work shall be made manifest, which is not until the next life. They shall be saved, indeed, by fire, that is, by passing first through Purgatory.

(I Cor 3:13-15) Protestants have interpreted this text to justify their claim of justification. First, Paul is not speaking of all men, only of teachers, and the quality of their work (teachings) will be judged. This text only says that some teachers' works will stand and some will not, and some teachers who make mistakes will also be saved.

(Matt 5:25-26) In this text Cyprian, one of the most ancient Church Fathers, means the prisons of Purgatory. He writes in his Epistle 52,

> Be at agreement with thy adversary, whilst thou are in the way with him, perhaps, the adversary delivers thee to the judge and the judge delivers thee to the officer, and thou be cast into prison. Amen, I say to thee thou shalt not go out from thence who you repay the last farthing.

Old Testament

Our clearest account of any reference to a state of purgation is in the Old Testament (Macc 2) and also Sirach 7:33. The words do imply a Jewish belief that sins can be forgiven after death, and at some time these sins must be cleansed for a soul to enter Heaven. There can be no dispute among scholars concerning the fact that it was written in the second century before Christ and, as such, witnesses to a belief held by many of the Jews at that time. Besides clear proof in Maccabee 2, read Sirach 7:33, as it advised "Withhold not your kindnesses from the dead." Can this text be anything but correct when it is recommending prayers for the dead, since the author phrases the two parts of the sentence in an equal manner that is: be generous to both the living and the dead?

Historical Evidence

If proof in Scripture is not enough, look to the reliable testimony of tradition; look to the inscription on the walls of the catacombs of Rome. Look also to the inscription on tombs of ancient cemeteries. Our earliest writings of the belief in Purgatory come from Tertullian before the end of the second century. There is also the great Origen, another witness to this belief. Augustine writes of the belief in one of his sermons. "The Universal Church carries on the tradition which has been handed down by our fathers, that of praying for those who have departed." Take note that he is saying he is witnessing to the antiquity of the belief in the middle place. Ambrose writes, "All that we offer to God in charity for the dead is changed into merit for ourselves and we shall find it increased a hundredfold after our death." Jerome writes, "The relief which we practice for the departed obtains for us a like mercy."

Finally, for those Protestants who still use the passage from Ezekiel 18:4, "The soul that sins, it shall die," to show there is no venial sin and no Purgatory, I say read John 5:17, "Every kind of wrongdoing is sin, but not every sin is deadly."

Indulgences

What does the Catholic Church mean by Indulgences? It is the debt of temporal punishment which may remain due upon account of our sins, after the sins themselves, as to the guilt and eternal punishment have already been remitted by contrition, confession, and absolution. From Scripture we know that there is a punishment often due upon account of our sins, after the sins themselves have been remitted. This appears in the case of King David (II Kings 2) where, although the prophet Nathan, upon his repentance, tells him "the Lord hath taken away thy sins," yet he denounces unto him many terrible punishments, which should be inflicted by reason of this sin.

Granting Indulgences

From Scripture we find that the power of granting indulgences was left by Christ to the Church. (Matt 16:19) "I will give to thee the keys of the Kingdom of Heaven and whatever thou shall bind on earth shall be bound also in Heaven." And we have instances in the Scripture of St. Paul's granting indulgence to the Corinthian, whom he had put under penance for incest (II Cor 2:10), "To whom you have pardoned anything, I pardon also; for what I have pardoned anything for your sakes, I have pardoned it in the person of Christ," that is, by the power and authority received from God.

Chapter 10

Confession

The Sacrament of Confession

"Receive Ye the Holy Spirit: whose sins you shall forgive, they are forgiven them; and whose sins you shall retain, they are retained." This power to forgive sins was not a personal gift, but transferred to the Church until the end of time. Just as sin was to continue, so, also, was forgiveness of sin until the end of time. By the above quoted text, Christ has made His pastors the judges of men's conscience with authority to forgive or retain sins. Now, no judge can pass sentence without having full knowledge of a man's conscience other than by their own confession. It was the obligation of the faithful to lay open the state of their conscience if they hoped to have their sins remitted. Unless the words are twisted, the simple reading of the text is obvious. Sin does exclude men from Heaven. Men, sin, and the power to forgive must exist until the end of time.

But, according to Protestant theology, the original Greek words of the text, "remitted" and "retained," should be translated in the perfect tense. Thus, it would indicate an action already performed. The text more accurately translated is, "If you forgive the sins of any, they have already been forgiven. If you retain the sins of any, they have already been retained." Do you see how the Catholic Church reverses the text given in the original? Furthermore, not even the Apostles had the power to forgive sin. Only God has this power.

Some of us have heard the Protestant accusations of confessing one's sins to a priest: the priest is only a man and only God can forgive sin. To begin with, the priest is not only a man but a mediator between God and man. After receiving the Sacrament of Holy Orders (becoming a priest), with its gift of grace, he becomes as Christ, the active human instrument through which the grace of God passes to others. With his holy responsibility, Christ lives in him and acts through him for the salvation of men.

Before looking into confession, we would be wise to define Holy Orders. This is the sacrament instituted by Christ, by which bishops and priests are consecrated to their respective functions and receive grace to discharge them. At the Last Supper, Christ made His Apostles priests by giving them the power to consecrate bread and wine into His body and blood: "Do this for a commemoration of Me." To which He added, after His resurrection, the power to forgive sins of the penitent. See, also, the words of Paul to Timothy, whom he had ordained priest by the imposition of hands: "Neglect not the grace that is in thee, which was given thee by prophecy, with the imposition of the hands of the priesthood."

Through faith, most Christians accept the fact that Baptism washes sins away and cleanses the soul. The pouring of water and using the words are done by a man, who is also an instrument of God. Although we cannot wash away sins, we act for God, with His divine power as called upon. The Sacrament of Penance, as well as the other sacraments, are all confirmed by the power of God through men. If God is truly present by your faith in baptism, then can we not say He is truly present in all our sacraments?

The Old Testament

In the Old Testament, which was a figure of the Law of Christ, those that were infected with leprosy, which was a figure of sin, where obliged to show themselves to the priest and subject themselves to judgment (Lev 13:14 and Matt 8:4). This, according to the Holy Fathers, was an emblem of the confession of sin in the sacrament of Penance. In the same law, a special confession of sins was expressly prescribed (Num 5:5-7).

> When a man or woman shall commit any of all
> the sins that men are wont to commit, and by

negligence shall have transgressed the commandment of the Lord, they shall confess their sins.

The same is prescribed in the New Testament.

The New Testament

"Confess, therefore, your sins one to another" that is, to the priests or elders of the Church, whom the Apostles ordered to be called. And this was evidently the practice of the first Christians. To confess your sins to a person who had no power to forgive would be useless. Hence, the precept here means that we must confess to men whom God has appointed and who, by their ordination and justification, have received the power of remitting sins in His name.

Forgiveness Comes Through a Priest

Again the question arises, why cannot the sinner go to God directly and obtain forgiveness? Answer: because God has determined that it is through confession to His priests and absolution given by the same priests that He will forgive our sins. We do not decide for ourselves how we shall obtain forgiveness any more than we decide for ourselves how we shall obtain God's salvation in the first place. Doesn't it make sense, when you think that God has made the priests of His Church the judges of men's conscience, and has also laid an obligation upon the faithful to lay open the state of their conscience to them, that if they hope to have their sins remitted it must be through His priests? Would God give His Church the power of retaining sins, much less the keys of the kingdom of Heaven, if such sins which exclude men from the kingdom of Heaven might be remitted independently of the keys of the Church?

Early Witnesses of Confession

In Christian history, the Church power to forgive sin is witnessed by most all the great writers. The first testimony of secret confession is offered by Origen (Ps 37: hom 2,6). Although in the early Church, confession was not as necessary as now, most Christians were faithful to the Church, even to facing death for Christ. Martyrdom was a way to wash all sins away.

Cyprian speaks of forgiveness of sins accomplished by priests, "As often as Christians fall into sin after baptismal, sin can be forgiven again." Clement of Alexandria distinguishes between sins committed before and after Baptism:

> The former are remitted at baptism; the latter are purged by discipline....The necessity of this purifying discipline is such that it does not take place in this life and must after death.

Ambrose writes, "God makes no distinction; He promised His mercy to all, and has conferred the power of forgiveness on all His priests without exception." All in all, Confession is another way to show our willingness to ask God for His forgiveness, and our desire to show our love to Him. Clement of Rome around 90 A.D. exhorted us to accept discipline to penance. Ignatius (107 A.D.) wrote, "The Lord forgives those who do penance." Polycarp wrote (156 A.D.) "To be genteel and merciful towards all not strict in judgment, knowing that we are all debtors of sin." The Teaching of the Twelve, before 100 A.D., exhorted confessing sins before celebrating the Eucharist.

Chapter 11
The Mass and the Sacraments

Published by Pope Pius IV

The Mass

Q. *What is the Catholic doctrine as to the Mass?*

A. That in the Mass there is offered to God a true, proper, and propitiatory sacrifice for the living and dead.

Q. *What do you mean by the Mass?*

A. The consecration and oblation of the body and blood of Christ under the sacramental veils or appearances of bread and wine; so that the Mass was instituted by Christ Himself at the Last Supper. Christ Himself said the first Mass, and ordained that His Apostles and their successors should do the like. "Do this for a commemoration of Me." (Luke 22)

Q. *What do you mean by propitiary sacrifice?*

A. A sacrifice for obtaining mercy, or by which God is moved to mercy.

Q. *How do you prove that the Mass is such a sacrifice?*

A. Because in the Mass, Christ Himself, as we have seen, is really present, and, by virtue of the consecration, is there exhibited and present to the eternal father under the sacramental veils, which by their separate consecration represent His death. Now, what can more move God to mercy than the oblation of His only Son, there really present, and under this figure of death representing to His Father that death which He suffered for us?

Q. *What Scripture do you bring for this?*
A. The words of consecration as they are related by St. Luke 22:19-20. "This is my body, which is given for you. This is the chalice, the New testament in My blood, which shall be shed for you." If the cup be shed for us, that is, for our sins, it must need be propitiatory, at least by applying to us the fruits of the bloody sacrifice of the cross.

Q. *What other text of Scripture do the fathers apply to the sacrifice of the Mass?*
A. The words of God in the first chapter of the prophet Malachi, where, rejecting the Jewish sacrifices, He declares His acceptance of that sacrifice, or pure offering, which should be made to Him in every place among the Gentiles. Secondly, those words of the Psalmist, "Thou art a priest forever according to the order of Melchisedech." Why according to the order of Melchisedech, say the holy fathers, but by reason of the sacrifice of the Eucharist prefigured by that bread and wine offered by Melchisedech?

Q. *What is the best method of hearing Mass?*
A. The Mass being instituted for a standing memorial of Christ's Death and Passion, and being in substance the same sacrifice as that which Christ offered upon the cross, because both the priest and the victim is the same Jesus Christ. There can be no better manner of hearing Mass, than by meditating on the Death and Passion of Christ, there represented; and putting one's self in the same disposition of faith, hope, charity, repentance, etc., as we should have endeavored to excite in ourselves had we been present at His passion and death on Mount Calvary.

Q. *What are the ends for which this sacrifice is offered to God?*
A. Principally these four, which both priests and people ought to have in view. (1) For God's own honor and glory. (2) In thanksgiving for all His blessings, conferred on us through Jesus

Christ our Lord. (3) In satisfaction for our sins through His blood. (4) For obtaining grace and all necessary blessings from God.

The Sacraments

Q. *What do you mean by the sacraments?*

A. An institution of Christ, consisting of some outward sign or ceremony, by which grace is given to the soul of the worthy receiver.

Q. *How many such sacraments do you find in the Scripture?*

A. These seven: Baptism, Confirmation, Eucharist, Penance, Extreme Unction (or the anointing of the sick), Holy Orders, and Matrimony.

Q. *What Scripture do you have for Baptism?*

A. John 3:5, "Unless a man be born again of water and the Holy Ghost, he cannot enter into the kingdom of God." and Matthew 28:19, "Going therefore, teach ye all nations; baptizing them in the name of the Father, and the Son, and the Holy Ghost."

Q. *How do you prove this commission given to the Apostles of baptizing Christians is to be understood of baptism administered in water?*

A. From the belief and practice of the Church of Christ in all ages, and of the Apostles themselves who administered baptism (Acts 8:36-38),

"See here is water," said the eunuch to St. Philip; "What doth hinder me from being baptized?" And they went down both into the water, both Philip and the eunuch; and he baptized him. (see also Acts 10:47-48)

Q. *What do you mean by Confirmation?*

A. Confirmation is a sacrament wherein, by the invocation of the Holy Ghost and the imposition of the hands of the Bishop with the unction of the holy chrism, a person receives the grace of the Holy Ghost, and a strength in order to the profession of his faith.

Q. *What Scripture have you for Confirmation?*

A. Acts 8:15-16, where Peter and John confirmed the Samaritans. "They prayed for them that they might receive the Holy Ghost; then they laid their hands upon them, and they received the Holy Ghost."

Q. *What have you for the Eucharist or Supper of the Lord?*

A. We have the history of the institution set down at large (Matt 26, Mark 14, Luke 22, I Cor 11) and that this sacrament was to be continued in the Church till the Lord comes, that is till the day of judgment, as we learn from St. Paul (I Cor 11:26).

Q. *What do you mean by the sacrament of Penance?*

A. The confession of sins, with a sincere repentance, and the priest's absolution.

Q. *What Scripture have you to prove that the bishop and priests of the Church have power to absolve the sinner that confesses his sins with a sincere repentance?*

A. John 20:22-23: "Receive ye the Holy Ghost: whose sins you shall forgive, they are forgiven them; and whose sins you shall retain, they are retained. Also, Matthew 18:18:

> Amen, I say to you, whatsoever you shall bind upon earth, shall be bound in heaven; and whatsoever you shall loose upon earth, shall be loosed also in heaven.
>
> Our Lord Jesus Christ, Who hath left power to His Church to absolve all sinners who truly repent and believe in Him, of His great mercy forgive thee thine offenses; and by His authority, committed to me, I absolve thee from all thy sins, in the name of the Father, and the Son, and of the Holy Ghost.

Q. *How do you prove from the text above quoted, of John 20:22-23 and Matthew 18:18, the necessity of the faithful confessing* *their sins to the pastors of the Church, in order to obtain the absolution and remission of them?*

A. Because in the text above quoted, Christ has made the pastors of His Church His judges in the court of conscience, with commission and authority to bind or loose, to forgive or retain sins, according to the merits of the cause and the disposition of the penitents. Now, as no judge can pass sentence without having a full knowledge of the cause, which cannot be had in this kind of cause, which regards men's consciences, but by their own confession, it clearly follows, that He Who has made the pastors of His Church the judges of men's consciences has also laid an obligation upon the faithful to lay open the state of their consciences to them, if they hope to have sins remitted. Nor would our Lord leave to His Church the power of retaining sins, much less the keys of the kingdom of heaven, if such sins as exclude men from the kingdom of heaven might be remitted independently of the keys of the Church.

Q. *What do you mean by Extreme Unction?*

A. You have both the full description an proof of it in James 5:14-15:

> Is any man sick among you? Let him bring in the priests of the Church, and let them pray over him, anointing him with oil in the name of the Lord. And the prayer of faith shall save the sick man, and the Lord shall raise him up; and, if he be in sins, they shall be forgiven him.

Q. *What is Holy Orders?*

A. A sacrament instituted by Christ, by which bishops, priests, etc., are consecrated to their respective functions, and receive grace to discharge them well.

Q. *When did Christ institute the sacrament of Holy Orders?*

A. At His Last Supper, when He made His Apostles priests by giving them the power of consecrating the bread and wine into His body and blood.

Q. *What Scripture proof have you that Holy Orders gives grace to those that receive them worthily?*

A. The words of St. Paul to Timothy, whom he had ordained priest by imposition of hands (II Tim 1:6), "Stir up the grace of God, which is in thee by the imposition of my hands;" and (I Tim 4:4), "Neglect not the grace that is in thee, which was given thee by prophecy, with the imposition of the hands of the priesthood."

Q. *When was Matrimony instituted?*

A. It was first instituted by God in Paradise between our first parents; and this institution was confirmed by Christ in the new law (Matt 19:4-6) where he concludes, "What God hath joined together let no man put asunder."

Q. *How do you prove that Matrimony is a sacrament?*

A. Because it is a conjunction made and sanctified by God Himself, and not to be dissolved by any power of man; as being a sacred sign or mysterious representation of the indissoluble union of Christ and His Church (Eph 5:31-32):

> For this cause shall a man leave his father and mother, and shall cleave to his wife, and they shall be two in one flesh. This is a great sacrament, but I speak in Christ and in the Church.

Q. *Why does not the Church allow of the marriage of the clergy?*

A. Because, upon their entering into Holy Orders, they make a vow or solemn promise to God and the Church to live continently. Now the breach of such a vow as this would be a great sin; witness St. Paul (I Tim 5:11-12) where, speaking of widows that are for marrying after having made such a vow as this, he says, they "have damnation, because they have cast off their first faith;" that is, their solemn engagement made to God.

Q. *But why does the Church receive none to Holy Orders but those that make this vow?*

A. Because she does not think it proper that they who, by their office and function, ought to be wholly devoted to the service of God and the care of souls, should be diverted from these duties by the distractions of a married life (I Cor 7:32-33)

> He that is without a wife is solicitous for the things that belong to the Lord, how he may please the Lord. But he that is with a wife, careth for the things that are of the world, how he may please his wife.

Q. *Why does the Church make use of so many ceremonies in the administering of the sacraments?*
A. To stir up devotion in the people, and reverence to the sacred mysteries; to instruct the faithful concerning the effects and grace given by the sacraments; and to perform things relating to God's honor and the salvation of souls, with a becoming decency.

Q. *Have you any warrant from Scripture for the use of such ceremonies?*
A. Yes; we have the example of Christ, Who frequently used the like ceremonies. For instance, in curing the man that was deaf and dumb (Mark 7:33); In curing him that was born blind; (John 9:6); and in breathing upon His Apostles, when He gave them the Holy Ghost (John 20:22).

Profession of Faith
Articles of the Church
Q. *What is your profession as to the articles of the Church?*
A. It is contained in the words of the Nicene Creed, "I believe in One, Holy, Catholic and Apostolic Church."

One
Q. *How do you prove that Christ's Church upon earth is always one?*

A. From many texts of Scripture. *Canticle of canticles*: "My dove, My undefiled, is but one—Fair as the moon, bright as the sun, terrible as an army set in array." John 10:16: "Other sheep I have, which are not of this fold," (the Gentiles who were then divided from the Jews,) "them also I must bring, and they shall hear My voice, and there shall be one fold, and one shepherd." Eph 4:4-5: "There is one body and one spirit, as you are called in one hope of your calling; one Lord, one faith, one baptism." In fine the Church of Christ is a kingdom which shall stand forever, and therefore must always be one; for "every kingdom divided against itself shall be made desolate, and every city or house divided against itself shall not stand" (Matt 12:15).

Holy

Q. *How do you prove this?*

A. First, because as we have seen above from Matthew, Our Lord, Who cannot tell us a lie, has promised that His Church should be built upon a rock, proof against all floods and storms, like the house of the wise builder, of whom He speaks (Matt 7:25) and that the gates of hell shall never prevail against it. Therefore the Church of Christ could never cease to be holy in Her doctrines, could never fall into idolatry, superstition, or any heretical errors whatsoever.

Secondly, because Christ, Who is the way, the truth, and the life, has promised to the pastors and teachers of His Church, to be with them always, even to the end of time. therefore they could never go astray by pernicious errors.

Thirdly, because our Lord has promised to the same teachers (John 14:16-17): "I will ask the Father, and He shall give you another Paraclete, that He may abide with you forever—The Spirit of Truth." In v16, He assures the teachers that this Spirit of Truth "will teach them all truths. How then could it be possible that the whole body of these pastors and teachers of the Church, who, by virtue of these promises, were to be forever guided into all truths by the Spirit of Truth, should at any time fall from the truth by errors in faith? (See also Isai 35:8, Isai 59:20-21, Isai 54:9-10, and I Tim 3:15.)

Catholic

Q. *What do you understand by this?*

A. Not only that the Church of Christ shall always be known by the name of Catholic, by which she is called in the creed, but that she shall also be truly Catholic, or universal, by being the Church of all ages and all nations.

Q. *How do you prove that the true Church of Christ must be the Church of all ages?*

A. Because the true Church of Christ must be that which had its beginning from Christ, and as He promised, was to continue until the end of the world.

Q. *How do you prove the true Church must be the Church of all nations?*

A. From many texts of Scripture, in which the true Church is always represented as a numerous congregation spread through the world. Gen 22:18: "In thy seed shall all the nations of the earth be blessed." Psalm 2:8: "Ask of Me, and I will give thee the Gentiles for thine inheritance, and the utmost parts of the earth for thy possession." Psalm 21:28: "And all the ends of the earth shall remember, and shall be converted to the Lord, and all the kindreds of the Gentiles shall adore in His sight. Isai 49:6: "It is a small thing that thou shouldst be My servant to raise up the tribes of Jacob. Behold I have given thee to be the light of the Gentiles, that thou mayst be My salvation even to the farthest parts of the earth." Isai 54:3:

> Give praise, O thou barren that bearest not; forth praise, and make a joyful noise, that thou didst not travail with child; for many are the children of the desolate, more than of her that hath a husband, saith the Lord. Enlarge the place of thy tent, and stretch out the skins of thy tabernacles. Spare not; lengthen thy cords and strengthen thy stakes. For thou shall pass the right hand and to the left; and thy seed shall inherit the Gentiles.

Mal 1:11: "From the rising of the sun even to the going down, My name is great among the Gentiles."

Apostolical

Q. *How do you prove this?*

A. First, because only those that can derive their line from the Apostles are the heirs of the Apostles; and consequently, they alone can claim a right to the Scriptures, to the administration of the Sacraments, or any share in the pastoral ministry. It is their proper inheritance, which they have received from the Apostles, and the Apostles from Christ.

Secondly, because Christ promised to the Apostles and their successors that "He would be with them always, even to the end of the world" (Matt 28:20). "And that the Holy Ghost, the Spirit of truth, should abide with them forever" (John 14:16-17).

The Ordinances and Constitution of the Church

Q. *Why do you make profession of admitting and embracing all the ordinances and constitutions of the Church?*

A. Because Christ has commanded, "He that heareth you, heareth Me; and he that despiseth you, despiseth me." As My Father hath sent Me, even so I send you." Hence, St. Paul tells us, "Obey your prelates, and be subject to them."

Q. *Why does the Church command so many holy days to be kept? Is it not enough to keep the Sunday holy?*

A. God, in the Old Law, did not ordain it enough to appoint the weekly Sabbath,which was the Saturday, but also ordained several other festivals, as that of the Passover, in memory of the delivery of His people from bondage, that of the weeks, or Pentecost, that of the Tabernacles, etc.; and the Church has done the same in the New Law, to celebrate the memory of the chief mysteries of our redemption, and to bless God in His Saints.

Q. *Is it not said in the Law (Exodus 20:9), "Six days shalt thou labor, and do all thy works?" Why then should the Church derogate from this part of the commandments?*

A. This was to be understood in case no holy day came in the week; otherwise the law would contradict itself, when in the 23d chapter of Leviticus, it appoints so many other holy days besides the Sabbath, with command to abstain form all servial works on them.

Q. *As to fasting days, so you look upon it as sinful to eat meat on these days without necessity?*

A. Yes; because it is a sin to disobey the Church. "If he neglect to hear the Church, let him be to thee as a heathen and a publican." (Matt 18:17)

Q. *Does not Christ say (Matt 15:11), "That which goeth into the mouth does not defile a man?"*

A. True; it is not any uncleanness in the meat (as many ancient heretics imagined) or any dirt or dust which may stick to it, by eating it without first washing the hands (of which case our Lord speaks in the texts here quoted), which can defile the soul; for every creature of God is good, and whatsoever corporal filth enters in at the mouth is cast forth into the draught; but that which defiles the soul, when a person eats meat on a fasting day, is the disobedience of the heart, in transgressing the precepts of the Church of God. In like manner, when Adam ate of the forbidden fruit, it was not the apple which entered in by the mouth, but the disobedience to the Law of God which defiled him.

Chapter 12
Apocalypse

The last of the Canonical books of the New Testament, The Apocalypse, was written by John the Apostle and Evangelist about 95-97 A.D. on the island of Patmos, to which he had been exiled by Emperor Domitian. Its twenty-two chapters can be divided as so: three addresses to seven bishops of cities in Asia Minor, fifteen on the persecution of the Church, four remaining on the triumph of the Church, the marriage of the Lamb, and the happiness of the triumphant Church.

"Apocalypse" is misleading. As an example of how misleading it is, we can see so often that we hear people refer to the book as "Revelations" that they are thinking in terms of "the shape of things to come." "Revelations" means the unveiling of secrets, and what is more secret than a future only God can know? It is unfortunate to think the book needs only to be read and interpreted. This way of thinking has brought out many erroneous interpretations. It is true that Revelations is the unveiling of something and even of a future something, not of the indefinite future, but of something that was to happen (soon). It is the triumph of Christ which is coming at the end of time; but it also refers to the here and now, as well as the past.

The Triumph of Christ can be spoken of as the past because once for all, through His life, death, and resurrection, He has conquered death and sin. But He has done so only to the extent that man accepts His salvation and lives by it. He has conquered the enemy, which no longer has power over one who is truly Christian. But men can fall under this power again and again if they reject Christ's grace. Hence the life of Christians in this world is a battle, characterized by both victories and defeats, and the ultimate triumph of Christ is reserved to the future, when this battle has been fought to its conclusion. Until the world of the Church is completed, Christ's victory is not complete. It was to assure his readers that this victory would be complete that the Book of Revelations was written.

We can divide the book in two parts. In the first, John addresses himself to the faithful of Asia, who were his special charge. The seven dioceses of Churches within his provinces were designated by seven candlesticks. The first part of the first chapter is strictly ethical and historic. The second portion, covering the remainder of the book from Chapter Four to the end, is prophetical. It describes, under various mystical forms, the stages through which the Church has to pass, especially the last period of her existence, the time of the Anti-Christ.

Fundamentalist Interpretation

Among Protestant churches there are quite different interpretations. Some believe that the Pope is the Anti-Christ, that John speaks of Rev.: "Look, it's right in the Bible, it even describes the way he will dress, read between the lines." "The end is near. The 144,000 Jews are about to be converted." Yet others will say, "The 144,000 is the exact number of heaven. Look for those who have the number 666 branded on their heads; the time will be here." They stand firm when they say, "World War III is about to begin" (the battle of Armageddon). "Don't you know that Ezekiel speaks of Gog and Magog (Russia and China)?" "Look also to 2 Peter, for he speaks of nuclear energy." *"Have you not read The Late Great Planet Earth?"* Accordingly, all these finalities are God's will, and man cannot change it. Christ will return and do it all; it's worthless to pray for peace. Everything is in His hands, such as the final cosmic battle. And this final battle will bring in the thousand-year reign.

There are many who claim that, under the inspiration of the Holy Spirit, they are able to understand the full text and its meaning. Some past and present preachers claim to know all there is to know concerning the end of the world, from John's Apocalypse.

Although it was not written to provide a blueprint by which a person of ingenuity could plot the course and destiny of peoples and nations down into the present time, people have tried and misused the Apocalypse in this way for countless generations, and invariably they have found its "revelations" playing out just as events reach their lifetimes.

Don't Be Fooled

In Luke 21:8 Jesus said,

> Watch out; don't be fooled, because many men will come in My name saying, I am He! and, the times has come! But don't follow them. Don't be afraid when you hear of wars and revelations. Such things must happen first, but they do not mean the end is near.

The Bible must be taken and understood by the devoted student of its complete works. Complete investigations of all the most learned scholars of the ancient world must be studied. Those who wish to preach and teach must know of the other books which were to inspire John's imagery. Among the Jewish apocalypse are the books of Henoch, the Apocalypse of Moses, and Abraham, the Twelve Patriarchs, the Assumption of Moses and others. Some of these books were written while John was on Patmos composing his Apocalypse, and some were written two centuries before Christ. To understand the meaning of the numbers used as symbols, you must know the ancient Hebrew meanings, from that time when our calculating systems had not yet been invented. The early Christians' literature borrowed somewhat from the ancient Hebrew symbolism. For Rome at that time was symbolically Babylon and Lucifer was symbolically the Devil, who was King of Babylon (Isai 14:12).

Why Was It Written?

Remember Apocalypse was not written to frighten us or to worry us but to console and strengthen our faith. One reason it was written is, as the Roman historians tell us, all the might of the Roman empire was used against the Christians as Nero used Christians as a scapegoat on which to lay the blame for the great fire of the city of Rome. Nero was murdered in 68 A.D. But the troubles of the Church were just beginning: the reigns of Vespasian (69-79 A.D.) and Titus (79-81 A.D.) and finally Domitian (81-96 A.D.), in whom all of Nero's wickedness was reincarnated against Christians.

The vision of Revelation comes in sevens, the number signifying totality or completion. The vision details the effects God's wrath will have on the sinful and upon the Roman Empire, which was then persecuting Christians. (Isai 25:8) "He will swallow up death for ever, and the Lord God will wipe away tears from all faces." Rev 21:4 reads, "He will wipe away every tear from their eyes, and death shall be no more." The learned and saintly Cornelis a Lapide by his understanding of Apocalypse is presented:

> The purpose of the Apostle, according to the author, is to animate the faithful of the apostolic age and all future time to invincible constancy in the faith, to the highest forms of holiness, and more particular to strengthen the witness with unflinching firmness.

For these Christians who were being persecuted by the Jews and oppressed by Rome, the suffering and torment of these first centuries were in need of hope. They needed the feeling that Heaven was not far from Earth. As the Martyrs of Christ increased, the Catacombs were filled with joy of hope and the knowledge of eternal happiness with Christ.

Another reason for John to write the Apocalypse was that during his time and long after even till this day, men such as Cerinthus and Ebion of the first century openly denied the divinity of Christ, although they called themselves His followers. They also taught that Christ, even as the Son of God, had no existence before the Blessed Virgin Mary. As it was John who was prepared to answer this heretical poison, he wrote and proclaimed, "In the beginning was the Word." So in the Apocalypse he makes Christ himself declare: "I am Alpha and Omega, the words meaning the beginning and the end...who is and was, and who is to come, the Almighty." John shows that the tree of the Church waves strong in all the fury of the tempest, and that for those who struggle here for the good cause there is laid up an eternal reward. It is this triumph of the just which he has described in Chapters 21 and 22.

Catholics do believe and proclaim the Lord will come again as in our prayers: "Thy kingdom come." Don't expect the ancient battle fields of Armageddon to come alive again. For we read in Luke 17, "The kingdom of God is not coming with signs to be observed; nor will they say, 'Lo, here it is!' or 'There for behold the kingdom of God is in the midst of you.'"

The Virgin Mother

It must be remembered that, just as the title "Virgin Mother" was given to the Church by the early Fathers, so we find them also applying the same prophetic passage of Scripture both to Christ's spouse the Church, and to His Virgin Mother, the Church being the virginal Mother of His children here below. It would then be natural for us to assume that she who is the parent of Christ, our Head, has all the concern for its members, and performs for them the works of a mother, of love and watchfulness, in all ages hence, the constant application now to the Church, and to Mary of that passage in Apoc 12:1:

> And a great sign appeared in Heaven, a woman clothed with the sun and the moon under her feet, and on her head a crown of twelve stars. And being with child, she cried traveling in birth, and was in pain to be delivered. And there was seen another sign in Heaven: and behold a great red dragon having seven heads and ten horns...And the dragon stood before the woman, who was ready to be delivered, that when she should be delivered, he might devour her son....And her son was taken up to God and

his throne. And there was a great battle in Heaven;
Michael his angel fought the dragon, and the dragon
fought with his angel.... And that great dragon was
cast out, that old serpent, who is called the Devil
and Satan, who seduces the world.

Irenaeus, 120-200 A.D., saw this conflict carrying out the idea
prophesied in Genesis, at the very beginning of revealed history,
described as it happened in the last half of the first century of
Christianity, and as it has continued down to our own day. The
Second Eve is foretold to the first in this passage:

I will put enmities between thee and the woman, and
thy seed and her seed shall crush thy head and thou
shalt lie in wait for her heel. To the woman also He
said: I will multiply thy sorrows... in sorrow shalt
thou bring forth children.

The enemy of God and mankind has never ceased from that day
till now to make war on God's children here below. In the Old Law
of the Church, which God established through Moses, amid what
sorrow did she bring forth sons to God! In the New Law, how the
battle has gone on, between the Church of Christ and the seven-
headed serpent of Heresy, ever watchful to devour each generation
of the Church. It is surely in sorrow, especially in our day, that the
Church brings forth her children, and she needs the embattled host
of Michael aiding her, to cast out the Old Serpent, the Adversary.

Spiritual Not Material
Things to Come

As you can see as you read Apocalypse, John used symbols to
convey his thoughts. Being a Jew, he knew the meaning of these
forms from earlier literature which he borrowed from. It is helpful
to try to understand the meaning of his ideas, not those he actually
describes in pictures, which his eyes did not see, but his thoughts.
It would be foolish to try to figure out how to open a scroll, sealed
with seven seals, and whether it can be opened a little at a time,

without breaking all the seals at once. The Prophecy of John is of spiritual not material things to come.

One thing that should be remembered is the biblical author did not have a scientific understanding of the world. As it was understood, earth was a flat dish floating on water ("the waters beneath the earth") (Gen 1:2, Job 28:14) anchored there by foundation pillars. Obviously this is not correct. So in the same way, Revelations speaks of heaven passing away as a scroll that is rolled up. The author is indicating the sky in the Old Testament conception, a kind of bowl inverted over the earth, hard and shiny. The word used is "firmament," which means something solid that has been beaten out and shaped. The sky is not really this, but the author thought of it that way. Remember that Jesus is described as a Lamb, a Bridegroom and a Son of Man. But these are symbols. Jesus is not really a lamb; neither is the "hundred and forty-four thousand" a precise number but a symbolism. Apocalypse is not a dream book of the future, giving precise information about historical events. Do not be fooled by those who claim to interpret God's revelation. Some claim to know the exact number of the population of Heaven, the symbolic 144,000 which is the four-square number of the symbolic twelve tribes of Israel. For those who predict the future of God's revelation, remember His words in Mark 13:32, "Of that day or hour no one knows, neither the Angels in Heaven nor the Son, but the Father only."

The Millennium

From the time of the Middle Ages, Protestants have held a belief in the millennium or a special period of 1,000 years. What has been accepted by some in each generation has resulted in complicated calculations of the date of the second coming of Christ. The millennium is one example of how some reject what was already known as far back as the early Church.

Augustine takes up the question of the symbolism of John's Revelations, and much has been made clear. Augustine says the millennial kingdom had actually started with the birth of Christ.

One Thousand Years
Augustine, *The City of God*, Book 20, Chapters 7 and 8

If a hundred is sometimes used for totality, as when the Lord said by way of promise to him that left all and followed Him, "He shall receive in this world a hundredfold;" of which the Apostles give, as it were an explanation when he says, "As having nothing, yet possessing all things," — for even of old it had been said, the whole world is the wealth of a believer, — with how much greater reason is a thousand put for totality, since it is the cube, while the other is only the square? For the same reason, we cannot better interpret the words of the Psalm, "He hath been mindful of His covenant forever, the word which He commanded to a thousand generations," than by understanding it to mean "to all generations."

Hence the Apostle says, "What have I to do judging them that are without? Do not judge them that are within?" "And the souls," says John, "of those who were slain for the testimony of Jesus and for the word of God," understanding what he afterwards says, "reigned with Christ a thousand years," that is, the souls of the martyrs not yet restored to their bodies. For the souls of the pious dead are not separated from the Church which, even now, is the kingdom of Christ; otherwise, there would be no remembrance made of them at the altar of God in the partaking of the body of Christ. "Therefore, while these thousand years run on, their souls reign with Him, though not yet in conjunction with their bodies."

Why Some Rejected Revelations
There are ancient and modern scholars rejecting the idea that John the Apostle wrote the Book of Revelations because, to them, his identity has never been determined. In Eusebius' book *Church History* (325 A.D.), we read the Apocalypse of John and why some did not accept it.

> For he says... "I, John who saw and heard these things," therefore that he was called John, I do not deny. And I agree also that it is the work of

a holy and inspired man. But I cannot readily admit that he was the Apostle. For I judge the person the Gospel and Epistle of John and the form of expression. the evangelist gives his name, but never speaks as if referring to himself, or as to another. Then he writes also an epistle. John to the seven churches which are in Asia, grace be with you, and peace. But the evangelist did not prefix his name. But neither in the reputed second or third epistle of John...does the name *John* appear. Instead there is written the anonymous phrase "the elder" but again later he states, "I John" but that he who wrote these things was called John must be believed, as he says it; but who he was does not appear. For he did not say, as often in the gospel, that he was the beloved disciple of the Lord, or the one who lay on His breast, or the brother of James, or the eye witness and hearer of the Lord. He would have spoken of these things if he had wished to show himself plainly. He speaks as our brother and companion and a witness of Jesus, and blessed because he had seen and heard the revelation. Anyone who examines carefully will find the phrases "the life," "the light," "turning from darkness," frequently accruing in both, also "truth," "grace," "joy," "the flesh and blood of our Lord," "the Judgment," "the forgiveness of sins," "the Devil," "of anti-Christ," and "promise of the Holy Spirit."

In fact, it is plainly to be seen that one and the same character marks the Gospel and the Epistle throughout. But the Apocalypse is different from these writings and foreign to them. I think he was some other than those in Asia as they say there are two monuments in Ephesus, each bearing the name of John. It is necessary to point this out here, for I would not have anyone think that I said these things in a spirit of ridicule, for I have said what I have only with the purpose of showing clearly the difference between the writings.

Universally Accepted A.D. 397

First we should be mindful of the fact that, up till the fourth century, there were many writings in existence that were not inspired. They were known as spurious writings, because their authorship was not known with certainty. Many of the different congregations of the Church were using these because the Church had not examined, as yet, the different writings, and had not yet determined which were genuine, that is, inspired, and which were not. Soon disputes arose about the writings being inspired or not.

The difficulty which is present concerning the authorship of the Book of Revelations was a matter of considerable discussion and contest in the early Church. Eusebius was one of the foremost of the early scholars who was not convinced that John the Apostle was the author of this book. But, finally the judgment of the Church decided that the Book of Revelations properly belonged in the canon of inspired books, and, as a secondary judgment, that John the Apostle was the author.

This determination was made at the Council of Bishops, in the year 397 A.D. at Hippo, Africa. After diligent study of this book and all others in the Canon, the bishops selected 46 books of the Old and 27 of the New Testaments. This decision was ratified by the Pope under the guidance of the Holy Spirit.

Symbols Used by John

John, who was a Jew, knew the meaning and background of the Jewish symbolism as it was used to keep his book unintelligible to those enemies hostile to Christians, as before it had confused enemies of the Jews.

Lamb	Jesus
Lamb with horns	Sign of power
Sword	Word of God

White	Sign of victory
Four Angels	God's power
Wings of the great eagle	Divine protection
Stars	Angels
Saints	Members of the church
Golden bowls of incense	Prayers of the Saints
Eagle wings	God's protection of New Israel
Marriage of the Lamb	The Church is the bride
Land	Right order
Water	Chaos
Babylon	Pagan Rome
Mark of the beast	Those who worship images
Beast (first)	Enemies of the Church
Beast (second)	Paganism (voice of Satan)
Dragon	Satan power in the beast
Anti-Christ	A power that will continue
Six	Number for imperfection
Six Six Six	Greatest imperfection
Six Six Six	Nero Caesar (presumed)
Star fallen	Satan
Keys	Power
Birds	Ill omen
Locusts	Worsening of time at hand
Eagle	Roman Empire
Harlot	Goddess of Rome
Seven	Number of perfection
Four plus three	Number of perfection
Twelve	Tribes of Israel
Horseman	Worsening of time at hand
White	For victory
Red	For blood
Black	For plague
Death	For death
7 plus 12	Fullness and completion
24 Elders	Old an New Covenants
Two Witnesses	Faithful who died

Seven Eyes	Seven spirits of God
Seven candlesticks	Seven Churches of Asia
Seven heads	Seven hills of Rome
Ten Kings (ten horns)	Kings of Rome
Ten Days	Indefinite number, days short time opposed to years
42 months, 3 1/2 years, 1260 days	Half of seven years of problem
In his mouth it is sweet	Word of God pleasant to receive
In his mouth it is bitter	Unpleasant to receive and keep
144,000	Heavenly number of perfection
1,000 years	When the Church life on earth has run its course (1000 does not mean exact amount of time)
Armageddon	In John's time it was already a symbol of a battleground where Kings were slain

"Apocalypse has as many mysteries as words, or rather mysteries in every word." — Jerome

Chapter 13
Luther, Calvin, Henry VIII

Father of Protestantism
Martin Luther (1483-1546)

Martin Luther was himself a priest. In 1517 he began his criticisms of indulgences, even though he had preached correctly on indulgences as recently as one year earlier. Within a short time he became a popular German champion. Rome became embarrassed by Luther's accusations; Pope Leo X was quite willing to compromise on matters of discipline and conduct, but doctrine was another thing. Catholic doctrine was not the Pope's to change at his discretion; rather, it was a sacred trust from Christ and the Apostles, which he must keep from error.

Luther taught that the sacraments were merely symbols to excite faith, but inconsistently he held that Baptism and the Eucharist were in some way necessary. Luther denounced the Mass. It appears in his own writing, he was taught to abolish the Mass by the father of lies. Now who would venture to follow this man, for he says his master in religion and teacher was the devil? Luther, the first preacher of the Protestant religion, had no marks of being moved by the Spirit of God. But he bore many badges of sin. His furious and violent temper could not stand the least contradiction of his understanding of Scripture, as witnessed by his friends.

Luther separated himself from all churches pure and impure, true or false. Therefore Luther and his friends must have separated themselves from the True Church.

Luther attacked one of the most famous Catholic theologians, St. Thomas Aquinas, a Saint and Doctor of the Church whose life was filled with learning and writing, as well as teaching. As before him another so-called reformer, Martin Bucer, exclaimed: "Suppress Thomas and I will destroy the Church." In 1520 Luther caused Thomas Aquinas' work *Summa of Theology* to be burnt in the public square at Wittenburg. It has been said, "The value of Thomas' writings is perhaps best attested by the hatred with which they have ever been regarded by heretics."

The true church, Luther explained, is invisible; also he preached his theory called "Justification by faith alone." Man's sins are his fault. As a consequence, man can in no way merit for any good works. Sin has so ruined man's nature that he can do nothing but sin, and to observe God's law becomes impossible; it is only to believe in God's mercy and His merits. For Luther, the Church was "Altogether in the spirit...entirely a spiritual thing...believed in but not seen...."

What is certain is that not till the time of Luther had his doctrine of justification ever been stated in any of the Church writings. His position was of new beliefs that he discovered. They had to appeal to Scripture, argue from Scripture and interpret from Scripture alone. He had to give argument against the original thoughts. Definitions had to be changed, such as Purgatory cannot be received upon "saving by fire" or "entering through much tribulation into the kingdom of God." Luther's principles were now above what had the seal of authority an universally accepted by all Christians.

Luther's name in religion was "Friar Augustine" for his devotion to St. Augustine. Luther preached the opposite of the Saint and great father of the Church, who said, "Who created you without your cooperation will not save you without your cooperation."

What Sort of Man He Was

Luther was a man who had broken the solemn oath he had made at the altar of God to live a pure, single and virginal life. He, with Sister Catharine, who also took the same oath, broke their promise to God and set up house together. History will bear witness also of his approval and scandalous dispensation, by which he allowed Philip Landgrave of Hess to have two wives at once, contrary to the gospel. From Luther's own pen, we learn he encouraged lust and breaking vows with God. He is found charging God with being the author of sin.

Newly Discovered Doctrine

After fifteen hundred years of Christ's Church, Luther's ingenuity discovered a new doctrine in Paul's writings (Rom 1-17, Gal 3-11): "The just man lives by faith." Luther in his mind found the word "faith" to mean personal salvation and justification. Thus faith had a new and untrue meaning: "justification." And from the Bible he was ready to offer his proof. Abandon all that the Church teaches, for it is now worthless. He was ready to lead souls to Heaven. In Luther's estimation man was totally corrupt. It was not long for Luther and his friends, who used the Bible as their guide, to begin a perpetual changing of doctrines and ideas. Much inconstancy now develops with the word of God.

Protestants were soon to divide from one another in faith. Different branches developed due to the fact that every man's private judgment is the ultimate judge of controversies, so then it became impossible for them to become one, united in religion.

Luther the Revolutionist

Without exaggeration, Luther is presented to us from the facts of history. And history tells us of his personality. He was not at all the Elder that Paul describes one should be; Luther was not at peace with himself, or content or happy. He was proud and contemptuous in his speech, and his letters contain vulgar and profane language. They seem to be written by a person who was mentally deranged. No one can exaggerate his ideals better than his own writings and those of his friends. Read Luther's words, and take into account those of God and compare. The Monk of Wittenburg referred to by his friends as the Pope of Wittenburg has contradicted Jesus, the Bible and our own common judgment.

Martin Luther (Wit. v 304)
There is a time to hear the Law and a time to despise the Law...let the Law be off and let the Gospel reign....But if you do not, you need not be troubled in your conscience, for the transgression of the Law cannot possibly condemn you.

Jesus Christ (Mat 19-17)
If thou will enter into life, keep the Commandments.

Martin Luther (Wit. ad 5,1573)
If Moses should attempt to intimidate you with his stupid Ten Commandments, tell him right out: Chase yourself to the Jews.

Luther taught that God or the devil ruled our lives, and we have no freedom of choice, although God and his Saints have told us differently. "Before man is life or death, good or evil; that which he shall choose shall be given him." (Eccl 15:18) Luther claimed himself to be a "Messenger of God," and "a defender of religious liberty." But do consider his hate and his lack of giving religious liberty to others.

To the Catholics (Wit. 1, 478)
To destroy the Papacy, everything is allowed against the deception and depravity of the Papacy.

To the Jews
Luther gives this advice: first set fire to their synagogues and schools, then their houses, take away their prayer books, forbid the rabbis to teach, deny them legal protection, take away their money. Treat them with all severity.

To the Anabaptist

Luther, in dismay at Anabaptist disorder, bid the civil authorities to "hem them down, slaughter and stab them, openly or in secret." One historian writes that more that 100,000 were killed.

Luther also wrote and preached against the successor of Peter. He writes "Antichrist" against the church founded by Jesus, "the mother of fornication." Luther also shows no respect for the institution of marriage, starting with our first parents, as opposed to the views of scripture.

Jesus (Matt 19:4)

What God hath joined together let no man put asunder.

Martin Luther (Wit. v. 123)

The husband may drive away his wife, God cares not.

God (John 2:9)

Anyone who does not stay with the teachings of Christ, but goes beyond it does not have God.

Martin Luther (Wit. II, 459)

I confess that I cannot forbid a person to marry several wives, for it does not contradict the Scriptures.

Luther's ways were not as Christ's teachings. He goes so far as to advise against prayer and fasting to rebuke temptation. He declares celibacy is impossible. Was Luther just too weak to accept what Christ has asked, to take up "your cross and follow Me?" Did Luther not read the words of John? John speaks of love, obedience, and work for your rewards in faith.

Sin
Martin Luther (Wit. IV, 188)

Oh, that I could paint sin in a fair light, so as to mock at the devil and make him see that I acknowledge no sin and I am not conscious of having committed any. I tell you we must put all the Ten Commandments, with which the devil tempts and plagues us so greatly, out of sight and out of mind. If the devil upbraids us with our sins and declares us to be deserving of death and hell, then we must say: I confess that I have merited death and hell but what then? Are you for that reason to be damned eternally? By no means. I know one who died and made satisfaction for me: Jesus Christ the Son of God. Where He is there also I shall be.

Free Will Is Not Lost
God Urges Us to Perfection

I cannot say whether anyone has reached perfection to their ability, but God does not give impossible commands. God would Himself be the author of injustice were He to demand the doing of what cannot possibly be done.

Jesus says: "Be perfect as your heavenly father is perfect."

Moses says: "Be perfect in the sight of the Lord your God."

Abraham says: "Be thou without spot and I will make My covenant between Me and thee."

God Urges Us to Pray

Jesus taught, "You should always pray and never become discouraged." Christ urged us to pray that we will not fall into temptation, quite the opposite of the teachings of Martin Luther.

In Scripture we refer everything to the will of God so we may be found worthy to receive that for which we pray. I say to you there is no place in Scripture which says free choice is lost. We sin or obey by our free will, and again we are warned by God (John 5:14): "Behold thou art made whole, sin no more lest a worst thing happen unto thee." But Luther said, "Put the Commandments out of sight and out of mind."

Before Luther deserted the Church, he himself seems to be describing himself.

Luther (Seidemann)

The principal sin of heretics is their pride....Frequently they serve God with great fervor, and they do not intend any evil; but they serve God according to their own will....They think they are guided by God....They interpret the Bible according to their own heads and their own particular views and carry their own opinions into it.

Paul to the Galations

Though we Apostles or even an angel from heaven were to come and preach to you a different Gospel from what we have preached, let him be anathema.

The words of Paul tell us religion must come from God, not from man. No man has a right to establish a religion; no man has a right to dictate to his fellow men what shall be believed, and what shall be done to save his soul. Religion must come from God, and anything else is but a human institution, not a divine institution.

Predestination
A New Doctrine Discovered by John Calvin

John Calvin set out to improve upon Lutheranism. Whereas Luther was chiefly concerned with the feeling that he was here and now justified before God, Calvin's cold logic carried the problem beyond time. What Calvin demanded was not merely certainty of present justification, but assurance of salvation hereafter. This point he settled to his own satisfaction by his doctrine of absolute predestination: from all eternity God by an unchangeable decree of His omnipotence will save or damn human souls, and there is nothing that men can do about it. Men, therefore, do not "receive" God's grace, but the elect may "perceive" that they are predestined.

The ultimate authority for all this is nothing but the infallible interpretation of Scripture by Calvin, for "God has designed," as he said, "to make known to me what is good and what is evil." And be it noted here that Calvin profited by Luther's embarrassment. Instead of conceding full private judgment to his followers, Calvin carefully explained the desired interpretations to his chief aides, who then passed them on to the people.

John Calvin's father and elder brother were laymen, both Church lawyers and treasurers of the bishopric of Noyon in Picardy, where he was born. Though Calvin himself was never ordained, he profited by the clerical system of his day. From the age of twelve, he enjoyed the revenues from established Church jobs without discharging his duties as either chaplain or pastor. These incomes financed his education at the University of Bourges-Orleans and Paris.

His father, Gerard, had been involved in financial difficulties with the Bishop of Noyon, for whom he was treasurer. Refusing to render his accounts, he had been excommunicated and, dying under blame and in dispute, he was denied church burial. Five or six years later, Calvin's elder brother, Charles, met a similar end. So there can be little doubt that he was embittered against ecclesiastical authority, whose hand had fallen heavily on his wayward relations.

On November 1 of 1533, Nicholas Cop, incoming rector of the University of Paris, delivered an address that in large part was "ghost written" by Calvin. This speech seems to have tried to claim that the Catholics held much the same view as Luther by comparing the most daring passages of the former with the least offensive of the latter. Two Lutheran ideas were stressed: (1) the opposition between the Gospel (of Luther) and the Law (of the Church); and (2) men's justification in the eyes of God by faith alone without good works. The speech seems to have been a trial to sound out the French king's sentiments towards the new religion.

The king began to arrest suspects as enemies of the state. Calvin, finding his native land too hot for him, soon became a refugee. He visited Germany and Italy before settling in Switzerland.

Calvin found a promising field open to him in Geneva, Switzerland. This town had long been at odds with its Bishops, who were both the spiritual and civil rulers, where a rebellion at first directed merely against the civil rule of the clergy ended by overthrowing spiritual authority as well. The Bishops of Geneva were usually nominees of the Duke of Savoy of the same noble family which ruled in Italy. Against this foreign rule, a group of Swiss patriots called "Libertines" had banded together to win independence. Like most rebels, they were not over-scrupulous about accepting allies.

Calvin's new type of "welfare church" was not established without difficulty. The Libertines, after all, had revolted in order to win liberty. In 1538 the Libertines won a majority in the council and exiled Calvin. But because of the Catholics' efforts to regain control, Calvin was invited to return to Geneva, where he remained supreme until his death in 1564. The Libertines continued in opposition until 1555 when death and exile had reduced their strength. For between 1546 and 1564 in a town of 20,000 inhabitants, there were 58 executions, 73 sentences of exile, and nine hundred of imprisonment. Thus the people of Geneva paid a high price for the authoritarian efficiency of John Calvin.

The Catholic Church Declares Against Calvin

The Council of Trent declared against Calvin, that certainty in regard to one's predestination can be attained by special revelation only. Holy Scripture tells us to work out our salvation in fear and trembling (Phil 2:12). He who imagines that he will stand should take care lest he fall (I Cor 10:12). In spite of this uncertainty, there are signs of Predetermination which would indicate high probability for one's predestination, such as preserving practice of the virtues recommended in the Eight Beatitudes, with an active love for one's neighbor and Christ and His Church.

The wars of religion were all over Europe. In France the political Calvinists were battling the political Catholics. Priests were killed in the thousands as the Calvinists were taught to hate Catholics as idolaters. Thousands of churches were sacked, their treasures of art stolen and the sacred relics of saints destroyed. How little did such a "reformation" resemble the first establishment of the Church of Christ. As already pointed out, there were good and bad on both sides of the religious wars. It seems that many in the Middle Ages were given over to these men who claimed new revelations from God. Could it be the wisdom of God to choose so many new and different beliefs by so many different men? Of course not. Christians were killing Christians. So now, across the channel to England and to what King Henry was to create, "The Church of England," mind you, not the Church of God but the Church of England. England was to become an absolute monarchial state, with the consolidation of royal power over the new national churches.

Henry VIII

Anglicanism was an original blend of Lutheran and Calvinist teaching and organization. When Pope Clements VII and the Catholic Supreme Marriage Court refused to allow King Henry VIII of England to divorce his wife of twenty years, in order to wed his mistress, Anne Boleyn, the king broke with the Roman Church. His own royal version of Christianity was set up by an "Act of Supremacy," November 1534, decreeing that

> Our sovereign Lord, his heirs and successors,
> kings of the realm, shall be taken, accepted, and
> reputed the only supreme head on earth of the
> Church of England.

An oath was exacted of important subjects. Sts John Fisher and Thomas More, bishop and chancellor, refused. The second distinguished: while Parliament might choose a king independently of the Pope's wishes, it could not regulate the Church; More was willing to accept Henry as king but not as Pope. But Henry put his critics to death and went on with his plans, which included seizure of most of the Church property for his own and his noble allies' profit. While Henry claimed to keep all other Catholic doctrines, after his death his ecclesiastical aide, Thomas Crammer, Primate of Canterbury, made decisive changes.

In the past England had been quick to accuse the Holy See of favoritism when French Popes resided at Avignon, France, and they had tried to arbitrate in the Hundred Years' War (1338-1453) between England and France. England had especially objected to receiving Italian appointees for English bishops' and clerical posts. This jealous desire of "England for the English" had never resulted in actual schism, but an almost ingrained sensitivity to "papal aggression" had developed.

Henry, Divorce Case

It is impossible here to go into all the details of he "divorce case" that was argued from 1527 to 1534. The facts of the matter are not seriously questioned by unbiased historians. Briefly, Henry demanded that Pope Clement declare his marriage with Catherine null and void; no marriage at all. The king stated that Pope Julius' dispensation was no good; he had exceeded his power. Such a claim was impertinent, for it seemed to question whether the Popes had really received Peter's power of binding and loosing, and whether they could be trusted not to fall into error.

As it turned out, the dispensation of Julius II was judged good. Christian teaching, moreover, permitted separation for a just cause, but not divorce with remarriage. Pope Clement, therefore, could not conscientiously grant what Henry asked, however much he would have liked to please his powerful petitioner and thereby save a nation for the Church. The Pope heard, however, from common gossip that Henry's real objective was a new wife, Anne Boleyn. Given time, Henry's passion for Anne might cool, as it had toward so many others in the past; then the king might abandon the case. The Pope delayed his unfavorable decision from year to year in the hope that Henry would master his passion.

But this time Henry was completely infatuated. He wanted his way at all cost; he had been accustomed by now to having it for twenty years. If the Pope would not give the annulment with permission to remarry freely, perhaps he could be bullied into doing so.

In 1529 the king began to urge the English Parliament to protest against excessive clerical fees, and in particular to threaten to cut off the papal revenues from England. The English bishops were blackmailed into recognizing Henry as "Supreme head of the Church and clergy of England." To be sure, the frightened prelates qualified their statement with the phrase, "so far as the law of Christ allows." But in their hearts, they must have been aware that for fifteen centuries the law of Christ had not included headship of the Church among the "things that are Caesar's."

When the Pope was finally obliged officially to deny Henry his annulment on March 24, 1534, the king was ready to strike back. Indeed his lust had maneuvered him into a position from which he could not retreat without loss of face or admission of guilt. For while his case was still pending at Rome, Henry had entered into relations with Anne Boleyn. When she had become pregnant, he had rushed through a quiet divorce and remarriage before his cursitor, Thomas Crammer, named Archbishop of Canterbury for just that purpose.

All ecclesiastical possessions now lay at the disposal of the new "Supreme Head of the English Church," and why should not his friends share in the pickings? Here also Henry's course seemed already marked out for him. His father's extended treasury had taught him extravagance, but now he had squandered it and needed more money. Parliament would grant new taxes, but probably with strings on them. The king's only way out was to take the wealth of the Church, especially that of the monasteries.

Confiscation of Church Properties

To excuse his confiscation, Henry made charges of clerical immorality which were either highly exaggerated or completely invented. A popular rising in defense of the monasteries, the "Pilgrimage of Grace" in 1536, was deceived, divided, and conquered by the king's diplomats and generals.

And so Henry took what he wanted. But at the same time, many of his aides also filled their pockets. Through royal negligence and extravagance, there lay continued separation from Rome. This group of newly-rich henceforth opposed reconciliation with the Pope lest this involve surrender of their stolen goods.

With Mary Tudor (1553-58), the royal will was once more Catholic, and Englishmen made no great difficulty in returning to their allegiance to the Pope. But then, Anne Boleyn's daughter, Queen Elizabeth I (1558-1603) once more changed the royal will, reaffirmed the doctrine of royal supremacy, and summoned weary Englishmen to yet another religious somersault.

Chapter 14
Church History

Christendom in the Dark Ages

In the Sixth Century, a new prophet was to appear; his name was Mahomet. His first act was to unite all the tribes of the desert and to wage a holy war to the end against Christians. This was God's revelation to him. Within ten years of his death, his followers overran all of the Persian Empire. Soon, all of Roman Africa was to fall to them. In 711, they conquered Spain and overran the south of France. They were also to lay siege to Constantinople. This was the siege of Christendom. The assault lasted for some nine hundred years.

In the East
Persecutions of the Bishops and Priests

The hero of the east who repulsed Mahometan was King Leo III. His religious policy was supreme in Church as well as state affairs. It was Leo who did away in the eastern churches with paying reverence to the images of saints. Riots soon began, and the imprisonment of clergy with the sentences of death followed. The Pope followed with a bold protest, and the emperor threatened with an invasion of Rome. By luck, the fleet sent to arrest the Pope was destroyed. Constantine V was to succeed Leo, and he showed himself to be even more bitter toward the Church. After the death of Constantine, the persecutions slackened. A council in 787 moved to restore the traditional Catholic teachings on the lawfulness of reverencing statues of the saints.

In the West
The Pope Becomes Temporal Ruler

Charles Martel was the hero of the West as Leo was of the East. His victory in Poitiers in 732 saved France and northern

Europe. He was the greatest emperor the West had seen for centuries, having united all of France. His son and successor was to continue the great work of restoring the west. With the Pope's sanction of the transfer of royal authority to his family, an alliance between the French people and the Papacy was destined. This ratification made the Popes temporal rulers of Italy.

For some fifty years, the Popes enjoyed the independence of any emperor. In the reign of Charlemagne (768-814), the Christian Prince began the work of restoration, and religious life was now in the care of the state. Although the reign of Charlemagne was good in one way, it was a problem in another. The emperor was to name the clergy as officers of state, and his son, Louis the Pious, began to name the Popes.

Church and State Collapse
(814-936)

Raids along the coast of France and Italy continued with the aggression of Mahometans. In 844, Rome was sacked and the tombs of the Apostles desecrated. Making matters even worse, pirates from the north (Denmark) were ferociously attacking Christians. Even England lay at the mercy of the new menace. This was the most serious setback since the Roman persecution of the Church. With no security of life, no strength to survive, people were in disorder. There was chaos and waste. The Church and State collapsed. There was no learning, so the clergy knew only the bare essentials of Church doctrines and sacramental practices. The tradition of holiness became rare. The Church was to be blamed for the wickedness of men. It was the circumstances of the time which brought about the nomination of clerics. Often in defiance of church law, they married and even transmitted their authority to their sons. This new lay domination with its wickedness did damage the image of the Church. In particular, the Pope had temporal rule over the city of Rome and the Papal state. Competition for the Papacy was sometimes competition for rival Roman families. It was a time when many Christian leaders were distracted from their spiritual concerns. It seemed at times the

Pope was not the Vicar of Christ, but only a petty ruler. In Germany also Prince Bishops combined spiritual and temporal authority and took part in politics and war.

Hope for the Church
(936-1002)

For a time there was hope for the Church, as Germany produced a great King, Otto I. Rome now had a new master. By luck the emperor was a good man and interested in religious reforms for the betterment of Christians. In his reign he kept a strict control over papal elections. His son Otto II and his grandson Otto III followed the same policy.

Another source of great strength for the movement of reforms came from the Benedictine monastery of Cluny in Burgundy. The new order was to rid itself of the abuse of prior centuries. The aim was to attract men by holiness and complete service to God. For the first time they were no longer under the jurisdiction of the bishop as many bishops were of little help in their job of saving souls.

For twenty more years the Church stayed independent of emperors, until the death of Pope Benedict. Succeeding Benedict was his brother, then his nephew. With them came even more scandals as renewed from the preceding century. Henry the III, a new emperor, wished to protect his own interest and marched on Rome. He removed the claimant to the papacy and nominated a new Pope, Clements II. Not until the death of Henry III, was the Pope duly elected by the clergy. A law was passed in 1059 to elect Popes by cardinals alone. It should be noted that the reform movement had made many enemies among these unlawful bishops and their families. In the first test, the cardinals elected the Bishop of Lucca, and the imperial court chose the Bishop of Parme. Three years the schism lasted, but the reforms had been established even though not perfected. The new Pope, Gregory VII, started a campaign to re-educate the clergy. He brought back celibacy and the old traditions. No more laymen were appointed to church offices. Excommunication was administered against those who disobeyed.

Henry IV Challenges the Papacy

Henry openly challenged the Pope for his appointment of the bishops. As for his rule, Henry felt he must have the power and support of the bishops. Therefore Henry deposed a present bishop and appointed another in his place. The battle of words began. Henry was at the height of his power but was ordered to Rome by a certain date, and if it failed, his soul would be condemned to hell. Henry then accused the Pope of adultery and the practice of magic. The Pope then issued a statement:

> I place King Henry...under interdict, forbidding
> him to rule in any of the kingdoms of Germany
> or Italy....I forbid that he be obeyed as King.

The King Appeals for Mercy

Henry's bishops were deserting him; other men who swore loyalty to him now had a reason to break their oath. Henry now felt his only recourse was to appeal to Pope Gregory's mercy. This he hoped to do as privately as possible.

January 28, 1077 marked one of the most famous events of history as Emperor Henry and Pope Gregory met at the Castle of Conossa. Henry's hopes for a private interview did not transpire. The Pope insisted on a public penance, which was common in medieval days. Henry had to beg forgiveness for three days before he was admitted to Gregory's presence. Pope Gregory then granted the pardon of which Henry begged. The Pope also withdrew his earlier statement against the King.

In time Henry continued his old policy of nominating the clergy, causing the Pope to renew the excommunication. Henry now marched on Rome to carry out the deposition of Gregory and to install his own elected Pope, Clements II. Henry died in 1106, as he was about to wage war on his son Henry, who also rebelled against him.

Italy Invaded by Frederick I Barbarossa

Pope Alexander (1159-1181) served the Church with no less than four claimants (anti-popes) to the chair of Peter. Emperor Frederick, refusing the election of Alexander, claimed all authority over Christendom, as Charlemagne had exercised. The war began in 1159, with the invasion of Italy and dragged on until the arm of the cities of Italy routed the Kings. Peace came in 1177, and Frederick finally acknowledged Alexander as Pope.

Francis of Assisi

One whom the Church will remember gratefully in the cause of reforms was Francis of Assisi, son of a wealthy merchant. Francis was one you would not expect to turn to God and give up a life of worldly pleasures. With only a handful of friends and a devotion to the Church and all it taught, Francis began to regain those who had fallen over to heresy. Within ten years he had five thousand followers, Friars. As priests joined them, they took to the study of theology. The importance of trained professional teachers is what the Church needed. From the blessings of Pope Innocent II, the Franciscans have continued to serve God.

Frederick of Sicily Claims All Authority

In 1213, a new King Frederick of Sicily was elected. This new emperor left no doubt that he was to rule the Church as well as his realm of Sicily. Even after his death in 1250, the war continued with his son Manfred, who inflicted heavy losses on the Pope's army. Charles, brother of Louis IX of France, was offered the throne of Sicily if he would come to the aid of the Church. The war ended in 1268, Charles now the new King of Sicily.

The Decline in France

The time of the decline was to begin from 1270 to the early 1500s. King Philip of France began to tax the Church and terrorized most into paying. The Pope forbade the payment of taxes and excommunicated any who paid and all who received the money. Finally the Pope did withdraw his demands, and for a few years there was an uneasy peace. Eventually there grew a new tension when Philip arrested the bishops. The king sent his army into Italy to capture the Pope. The French entered the Papal palace, and did capture him. But while debating whether to kill the Pope or abduct him to France, the people rose against the invaders. The French were driven out of the city. King Philip had done the unthinkable. Not only defying the Pope, he also brought down the prestigious power of the Church. The State was now the authority over Christendom.

The Decline in Germany

The death of Henry VII caused more problems in 1347. The leaders (Princes) of Germany were unable to agree on a new emperor. The Church rose to make the decision to rule during the vacancy. Germany was again at war; two rivals were fighting for the throne, Lewis of Bavaria and Frederick of Austria. Lewis invaded Italy, accused the Pope of heresy and treachery, and elected his own anti-pope as the new successor.

It should be mentioned the catastrophe of 1347, the bubonic plague, was sweeping the continent. This plague caused the death of millions; some estimates were one-third of the population. It seems that no one suffered more than the clergy. The replacements were very often filled by untrained and unsuitable subjects.

The Great Western Schism

The years between 1378 and 1417 produced more anti-popes. It should be pointed out that the Catholic Church has always recognized the Pope who resided in Rome, during the time of these rivals to the chair of Peter. Even though both were recognized and elected by the same body of Cardinals, the question arises, who is the real Pope? How did all this happen?

For more than sixty years, the Pope resided in Avignon, France. This was the time of the Hundred Years War between England and France. Rome, at this time, was not considered a safe place for anybody; but in 1367, the people of Rome could actually see their Bishop. The Pope stayed for three years and then returned to Avignon, France.

In 1370, there was to be a new election, and the cardinals were almost all Frenchmen. They elected Gregory XI, who returned to Rome after many political obstacles but soon died. Of the new election the cardinals were all but five of the sixteen Frenchmen. The French cardinals feared for their lives for around the Vatican came screams of the people to "Elect an Italian or you die." And so it was an Italian was to succeed, the first in seventy-four years. He took the name of Urban VI. Soon after the French cardinals escaped to France, they made an announcement that Urban VI was not the Pope. Their decision was made simply to escape death. With the aid of the French King, the French cardinals proceeded to have a new election without the Italians voting. They chose Clement VII. Christendom was now divided by two Popes elected by the same body of cardinals. The Church was now divided for almost forty years. It was not until the successors of both rivals were cited to appear at a general council representing the whole universal Church that this council put an end to the schism. Both Popes refused to attend, and in their absence the cardinals elected Alexander V. Alexander lasted only three months. His successor was to be John XXIII, one who seemed to have been a pirate and a trader of indulgences.

Three Claimants to the Papacy

It was now Emperor Sigismund who would end this division once and for all. In 1414 a new council was called in which more than 100,000 attended, including 185 bishops, 300 theologians, and almost 20,000 ecclesiastics. Alexander was deposed on charges of maladministration of Church property. Gregory decided to recognize the council. There still remained the successor of the one who started it all; but his support was not worth worrying about.

On November 11, 1417, the conclave of Cardinals elected a Pope, the Cardinal Odo Colonna. He took the name of Martin V.

The schism was now ended and the Church was united in obedience to Pope Martin V.

The Middle Ages

What put Christendom to sleep is a long story and cannot be told completely here. The basic cause was many churchmen had become too important for the good of the Church. These men were only human agents, holding indispensable offices in constant demand for advice on almost every subject.

Not that popes and bishops ever actually held the offices of emperors and kings, but they sometimes became so absorbed in teaching the latter duties in this life they came to neglect their chief concern of guiding souls to heaven. It was in the Dark Ages that the civil rulers felt the need to entrust some civil tasks to the only educated class, the clergy.

The Middle Ages was a time when the clergy were participating in worldly affairs. Many times there were movements to exclude bishops and clerics from politics. So began a new class of laymen who went far beyond their limits; they could not vote out the clergy as they saw fit. They had no direct grievance against any of the Church doctrines, so they began to toy with certain unorthodox opinions only to attack the clergy. Men such as Wycliff and Hus came forward to deny the authority of Rome. They preached that the sacraments, especially Holy Communion and Holy Orders, were not necessary.

Hus became a Protestant hero and martyr for the Czech people in particular. Hus accepted the anti-pope Alexander and stood ground on private judgment. The Archbishop of Prague adhered to Pope Gregory. Hus was able to maintain himself for a while with the support of King Wenceslaus. He continued writing on reforming the Church. A safe conduct was given to Hus if he would attend the Great council of Constance, where he could defend himself. He was not given protection according to testimony and condemned to die at the stake. Hus was condemned as a heretic and spiritually condemned by his own Archbishop. It must be understood the whole situation was involved in a conflict of church and state in which not only Hungary but Austria was involved. In view of the political situation, tough measures by the secular arm were taken in putting Hus to death.

Christians Battle Christians

Catholics and Protestants were battling all over Europe. Years were filled with hatred, death and massacres in the thousands. Priests were hated and considered to be idol worshipers. Priests were being killed by the new fierce protesters of Rome. "Besides innumerable other outrages, the reformed gospelers destroyed no less than twenty thousand churches," (*Jerusalem and Babel*). This was a time when priests and monks were changing their way of thinking and taught what they decided was right or wrong. Tradition was removed, such as the use of organs in Church, for it was not to be found in Scripture. Pilgrimages were preached against because they could not be found in Scripture.

Keep in mind, in these days men still believed the earth was flat and the center of the universe. Philosophers were beginning to attack theologians with a new daring wit, sometimes resorting to namecalling instead of honest argument. The clergy would be abusing the weak, and these personal attacks would develop into the attacks on the doctrines of the Church. There were now intellectuals who were discussing matters with the clergy and confusion was with the uneducated priests and monks. There were no sound answers for the valid criticisms and objections on Church teachings. Sound reason was to give way to true faith. There were many reasons that led to the great reformers of the Middle Ages. Bishops and priests were usually unavailable for information and comment, as they did not reside in their dioceses or parishes. This absenteeism caused much neglect for local situations. Monasteries had laymen elected for local abbots which resulted in spiritual mismanagement.

Prince Bishops and Unordained Cardinals

The idea of a Prince Bishop is so far from our state of mind and culture that it is hard for us to put the idea together. It is useful to remember that in the Middle Ages and thereafter, the noble families often did their best to get some of their members into the higher ranks of the clergy, thus increasing their influence in state affairs. In some cases these men made the royal course of study in preparation for the priesthood. In other cases they advanced without sufficient preparation. They were Princes or members of the higher nobility before they were accepted in the clerical order. In many instances because of royal connections, they were immediately advanced to higher offices in the Church. You can see how this situation could lead to grave abuses. In many cases there were ordained priests, still holding their title as nobles. Some cardinals had the title simply as an honor, while others were named to the offices and were actually advisers to the Pope. Of course, nowadays, only bishops are named to the office of cardinal.

Unity was to Explode

Christendom of the Dark and Middle Ages was now only united in appearance, for the great relaxing slumber was to explode with such great reformers as Luther, Calvin, and Henry the VIII. Although they were ancient pretenders to reformation, those who undertook to alter Church doctrines were condemned by the ancient Church as heretics and are acknowledged by the Protestants themselves. Therefore there is just reason to say they walked in the same path.

The Catholic Reformation

The Lutheran revolt was a shock, but far in the north. Perhaps what really brought the papal court into thought of reforms was the sack of Rome in 1527 by mutinous Imperial troops. Some feel it was a judgment of God on the abuses and confusion which had too long been tolerated in papal and episcopal administration.

Paul III (1534-49) was to succeed in breaking through the dull weight of custom. He filled the College of Cardinals and the Curia with a majority of able and moral prelates, and sponsored a commission which during 1536-37 studied the causes of the Catholic paralysis that had provoked the Protestant revolution.

This commission gave its verdict frankly: Holy father, it was the fault of the canonists, the curial lawyers. In particular, abuses were seen in (1) exaggeration of papal powers, with frequent sales of offices and other favors; (2) laxity in standards for admission to offices; (3) nomination of the unfit for offices; (4) holding of two or more offices that were incompatible, also pensions from patrons, rebates, absenteeism; (5) excessive exemption for religious orders resulting in controversies between parish and religious clergy; (6) disregard of supervision of schools, academies, and books; (7) abuse of dispensation that let down discipline through the indulgence of friends.

Pope Paul then set up a standing commission to follow up the reforms of these abuses. Beginning in 1542, he and his successors courageously and perseveringly proceeded with an overhauling of the papal court. Abuses slowed and indulgences were curbed; vigilance over doctrine and books was restored; new institutions were set up for the training of the clergy and teachers; revenues were cut and supervised; absenteeism and negligence were corrected. Eventually by 1587 a completely reorganized and departmentalized Papal Curia had emerged. Long before, however, Paul III had defied conciliarism by summoning the reforming Council of Trent.

The Council of Trent

The Council of Trent (1545-1563) probably faced the most difficult task of any general synod in history. It was obliged to lay down extensive plans for a restored Church organization while putting out the fire of "ecclesiastical anarchy." Unfortunately the wars of so-called Christian princes delayed the opening of the council until a generation after the Lutheran outbreaks. Though Lutherans were invited to take part in the discussion, by this time they had so long gone their separate way that they no longer considered themselves Catholics. Years of argument and even physical violence had diminished chances for calm discussion. Accordingly the Council had to go on by itself. Doctrinally the Council of Trent, like all its predecessors, professed reverence for both Scripture and tradition as interpreted in the living teaching authority of the Catholic Church under the guidance of the Holy Spirit. The list of divinely inspired books was reaffirmed; the existing Vulgate version of the Bible was declared free from doctrinal errors, though incidental mistakes of copyists might call for a textual revision.

In disciplinary matters, the Council of Trent affected considerable overhauling. The primacy of the Pope, with the need for a centralized and somewhat internationalized Curia of Cardinals and their aides was recognized. It was noted, moreover, that members ought to be of exemplary character and abilities. Bishops, even though of divine institution, were properly chosen or approved by the Holy See. Bishops ought to take care to reside habitually in their dioceses, to have personal concern in supervising the fidelity of their clergy—not excluding religious in matters pertaining to the care of souls—and they ought to instruct all of their flock by means of sermons. Particularly, they were reminded to be conscientious in selecting worthy candidates for ordination and ecclesiastical office.

Chapter 15
Ancient Church Writings

Witness to the Truth

The remainder of this book will include some of the writings of the early Church fathers. From them the Roman and Greek Churches received much of its information. They give us proof of the ancient Church tradition and its early history. Before the year 200, there were preserved about one hundred separate collections of Christians' writings. Part of this valuable collection of information comes from those who listen to the words of the Apostles and those who were taught by these first-hand listeners. Like many of the Apostles, they also were martyred for Christ.

Clements of Rome (?-97), Baptized by Peter; also knew Paul.
Ignatius of Antioch (?-107) Disciple of John; friend of Peter.
Polycarp (69-155) Disciple of John.
Justin Martyr (100-163) Lay writer of Christianity.
Ireaneus (125-203) Student of Polycarp.

Fourth Century

Eusebius (260-340) First Christian Historian.
Augustine (354-430) Writer of Theology and Philosophy.

Clements of Rome (?-97)

After the death of the Apostles Peter and Paul, Clements was to succeed eventually to the chair of Peter. Clements wrote in his Epistle to the Corinthians with the authority of an Apostle. Who was this man Clements? Most scholars agree that he is the one mentioned in Paul's writings (Phil 4-3). According to Eusebius, early Church historian, the Church help his Epistle in great esteem:

> There is one acknowledged Epistle of Clements (whom he has just identified with the friend of Paul), great and admirable, which he wrote in the name of the Church of Rome to the Church of Corinth, sedition having then arisen in the latter Church. We are aware that this Epistle has been publicly read in very many churches both in old times, and also in our day.

So this shows that this epistle was almost on a level with the inspired writings. And it is placed in the Alexandrian MS, immediately following the inspired books. It is in great harmony with the position thus assigned it by primitive Churches.

Epistle of Clements to the Corinthians
(68 or 69 A.D.)
Chapter XXXII

We Are Justified Not by Our Own works, But by Faith

Whosoever will candidly consider each particular, will recognize the greatness of the gifts which were given by him. For from him have sprung the priests and all the Levites who minister at the altar of God. From him also was descended our Lord Jesus Christ according to the flesh. From Him arose kings, princes, and rulers of the race of Judah. Nor are His other tribes in small glory, inasmuch as God had promised, "Thy seed shall be as the stars of heaven." All these, therefore, were highly honored, and made great, not for their own sake, or for their works, or for the righteousness which they wrought, but through the operation of His will. And we, too, being called by His will in Christ Jesus, are not justified by ourselves nor by our own wisdom, or understanding, or godliness, or works which we have wrought in holiness of hearts; but by that faith through which, from the beginning, Almighty God has justified all men; to whom be glory forever and ever. Amen.

Chapter XXXIV
Great Are the Rewards of Good Words with God

The good servant receives the bread of his labor with confidence; the lazy and slothful looks his employer in the face. It is requisite, therefore, that we be prompt in the practice of well-doings; for of Him are all things. And thus He forewarns us: "Behold, the Lord cometh, and His reward is before His face, to render to every man according to his works." He exhorts us, therefore, with our whole heart to attend to this, that we be not lazy or slothful in any good works. Let our boasting and our confidence be in Him. Let us submit ourselves to His will. Let us consider the whole multitude of His Angels, how they stand ready to minister to His will. For the Scriptures say:

> Ten thousand times ten thousand ministered unto Him, and cried, Holy, holy, holy is the Lord of Sabaoth; the whole creation is full of His glory....

Chapter XLII
The Order of Ministers in the Church

The Apostles have preached the Gospel to us from the Lord Jesus Christ; Jesus Christ has done so from God. Christ therefore was sent forth by God, and the Apostles by Christ. Both these appointments, then, were made in an orderly way, according to the will of God. Having therefore received their orders, and being fully assured by the resurrection of our Lord Jesus Christ, and establishment in the word of God, with full assurance of the Holy Ghost, they went forth proclaiming that the kingdom of God was at hand. And thus preaching through countries and cities, they appointed the first fruits of their labors, having first proved them by the Spirit, to be bishops and deacons of those who should afterward believe. Nor was this any new thing, since indeed many ages before it was written concerning bishops and deacons,

> For thus saith the Scriptures in a certain place,
> "I will appoint their bishops in righteousness,
> and their deacons in faith."

Chapter XLIV
The Ordinances of the Apostles Respecting Priestly Offices

Our Apostles also knew, through our Lord Jesus Christ, there would be strife on account of the office of the episcopate. For this reason, therefore, insomuch as they had obtained a perfect fore-knowledge of this, they appointed those ministers already mentioned, and afterwards gave instructions, that when these should fall asleep, other approved men should succeed them in their ministry. We are of opinion, therefore, that those appointed by them, or afterwards by other eminent men, with the consent of the whole Church, and who have blamelessly served the flock of Christ in a humble, peaceable, and disinterested spirit, and have for a long time possessed the good opinion of all, cannot be justly dismissed from the ministry. For our sin is great, if we eject from the episcopate those who have blamelessly and wholly fulfilled its duties....

Chapter LXII
Let the Authors of Sedition Submit Themselves

Ye therefore, who laid the foundation of this sedition, submit yourselves to the presbyters, and receive correction so as to repent, bending the knees of your hearts. Learn to be subject, laying aside the proud and arrogant self-confidence of your tongue. For it is better for you that ye should occupy a humble but honorable place in the flock of Christ, than that, being highly exalted, ye should be cast out from the home of His people. For thus speaketh all virtuous Wisdom:

> Behold, I will bring forth to you the words of My Spirit, and I will teach you My speech. Since I called, and ye did not hear; I held forth My words, and ye regarded not, but set at naught My councils, and yielded not at My reproofs; therefore I too will laugh at your destruction; yea, I will rejoice when ruin cometh upon you, and sudden confusion overtakes you, when overturning presents itself like a tempest, or when tribulation and oppression fall upon you. For it shall come to pass that when ye call upon Me, I will not hear you; the wicked shall seek Me, and they shall not find Me. For they hated wisdom, and did not choose the fear of the Lord; nor would they listen to My counsels, but despised My reproofs. Wherefore they shall eat the fruits of their own way, and they shall be filled with their own ungodliness....

Ignatius of Antioch (?-107)

According to Eusebius, Fourth Century historian, Ignatius was third bishop of Antioch. During his trip to Rome to be martyred, he wrote seven letters. The authenticity of the seven letters is widely accepted, and they are included among the Apostolic Fathers' writings. Legend has him appointed Bishop by Peter after Peter left the deathbed of Evodius, previous Bishop of the See of Antioch. His letters of instruction on the Church cover the Trinity, Incarnation, Redemption, and the Eucharist. Ignatius's writings are important among the early Christian writings as he received his instructions first-hand from the Apostles.

Quotes from the Seven Letters of Ignatius

"It is therefore fitting that you should by all means glorify Jesus Christ who hath glorified you: that by a uniform obedience ye may be perfectly joined together, in the same mind and in the same judgment: and all may speak the same things concerning everything. And that being subject to your Bishop, and the presbytery, ye may be wholly and thoroughly sanctified.

"For even Jesus Christ, our inseparable life, is sent by the Father; as the Bishop, appointed unto the utmost bounds of the earth, is by the will of Jesus Christ. Wherefore it will become you to run together according to the will of the Bishop, as also ye do.

"Let no man deceive himself; if a man be not within the altar, he is deprived of the bread of God. For if the prayers of one or two be of such force, as we are told; how much more powerful shall that of the Bishop and the whole Church be? He therefore does not come together in the same place with it, is proud and has already condemned himself.

"Pray also without ceasing for other men: for there is hope of redemption in them. Be ye mild at their anger; humble at their boasting; to their blasphemies return your prayers; to their error your firmness in faith; when they are cruel, be gentle; not endeavoring to intimate their ways.

"Obeying your Bishop and the presbytery with an entire affection; breaking one and the same bread, which is the immortality; our antidote that we should not die, but live forever in Christ.

"I desire the bread of God, which is the flesh of Jesus Christ, of the seed of David; and the drink that I long for is his blood, which is incorruptible.

"Wherefore as becomes the children both of the light and trust, flee division and false doctrines; but where your shepherd is there do ye, as sheep, follow after.

"Wherefore let it be your endeavor to partake all of the same Holy Eucharist. For there is but one flesh of our Lord Jesus Christ; and one cup in the unity of his blood; one altar, deacons my fellow servants, that so whatsoever ye do, ye may do it according to the will of God.

"And when he came to those who were with Peter, he said unto them, "Take, handle me and see that I am not an incorporeal demon." And straightaway they felt and believed; being convinced both by his flesh and spirit. But after his resurrection, he did eat and drink with them, as he was flesh; although as to his spirit He was united to the Father. "But I arm you beforehand against certain beasts in the form of men, whom you must not receive, but if it be possible must not meet with.

"But consider those who are of a different opinion from us, as to what concerns the grace of Jesus Christ which is come unto us, how contrary they are to the design of God.

"They have no regard to charity, no care of the widow, the fatherless, and the oppressed of the bond or free, of the hungry or thirsty.

"They abstain from the Eucharist, and from the public office; because they confess not the Eucharist to be the flesh of our Savior Jesus Christ, which suffered for our sins and which the Father of his goodness raised again from the dead.

"But flee all divisions, as the beginning of evils.

"Let that Eucharist be looked upon as well established, which is either offered by the Bishop, or by him the Bishop has given his consent. Wheresoever the Bishop shall appear, there let the people also be: as where Jesus Christ is, there is the Catholic Church.

"In like manner let us reverence the deacons as Jesus Christ; and the Bishop as the father; and the presbyters as the Sanhedren (supreme Jewish Court of justice) of God and college of the Apostles. Without these there is no Church. Fare ye well in Jesus Christ, being subject to your bishop as to the command of God, and so likewise to the presbytery."

To the Church That is in Rome
To the Church that is beloved and enlightened through the will of Him Who has willed all things that are according to the love of Jesus Christ our Lord, even to her that presides in the region of the Romans, worthy of God, worthy of honor, worthy of blessings, worthy of praise, worthy of prosperity, worthy in her purity and presiding over the brotherhood.

See how Ignatius writes with a different style with respect to the authority of Rome. As already stated, Ignatius was by legend a convert of John and appointed Bishop of Antioch by Peter. He was Bishop for forty years before being arrested. Now if anyone could set up a rival claim against the leadership of the Bishop of Rome, it would be the Bishop of Antioch, where Peter labored for years. Ignatius by far shows no authority over the Church of Rome. He writes,

Not like Peter and Paul do I issue any orders to you. They were Apostles; I am a convict; they were free; I am until this moment a servant.

Polycarp of Smyrna (69-155)

A letter to Polycarp from the Apostle John has survived, as has his "Epistle to the Philippians", in which he quotes from John 4:3 and warns against false teachings. Polycarp was reputedly the leading Christian in Roman Asia. The "Martyruim Polycarp", written in the name of the Church of Smyrna from eyewitness accounts of his arrest, trial, and death, is the oldest authentic account of the acts of a martyr.

His pupil Irenaeus reminisced:

> I could describe the very place in which the blessed Polycarp sat and taught; his going out and coming in; the whole tenor of his life; his personal appearance; how he would speak of the conversation he had held with John the Apostle and with others who had seen the Lord. How he did make mention of their words and of whatever he had heard from them respecting the Lord.

Polycarp writes like the beloved Apostle himself; nothing can be more clear than his view of the doctrines of grace.

Polycarp to the Philippians
Chapter VI
The Duties of Presbyters and Others

And let the presbyters be compassionate and merciful to all, bringing back those that wander, visiting the sick, and not neglecting the widow, the orphan, or the poor, but always "providing of that which is becoming in the sight of God and man;" abstaining from all wrath in respect of persons and unjust judgment; keeping far off from all covetousness, not quickly crediting an evil report against anyone, not severe in judgment, as knowing that we are all under a debt of sin. If then we entrust the Lord to forgive us, we ought also ourselves to forgive; for we are before the eyes of our Lord and God, and "we must all appear at the judgment seat of

Christ, and must everyone give an account of himself." Let us then serve Him in fear, and with all reverence, even as He Himself has commanded us, and as the Apostles who preached before-hand the coming of the Lord have alike taught us. Let us be zealous in the pursuit of that which is good, keeping ourselves from the causes of offense, from false brethren, and from those who in hypocrisy bear the name of the Lord, and draw away vain men into error.

Chapter VII
Avoid the Docetae, and Preserve in Fasting and Prayer
"For whosoever does not confess that Jesus Christ has come in the flesh is antichrist;" and whosoever does not confess the testimony of the cross is of the devil; and whosoever perverts the oracles of the Lord to his own lusts, and says that there is neither a resurrection nor a judgment, he is the first-born of Satan. Wherefore, forsaking the vanity of many, and their false doc-trines, let us return to the word which has been handed down to us from the beginning: "watching unto prayer," and preserving in fasting; beseeching in our supplication the all-seeing God "not to lead us into temptation," as the Lord has said: "The spirit is willing, but the flesh is weak."

Chapter XII
Exhortation to Various Graces
It is declared then in these Scriptures, "Be ye angry, and sin not," and, "Let not the sun go down upon your wrath." Happy is he who remembers this, which I believe to be the case with you. But may the God and Father of our Lord Jesus Christ, and Jesus Christ Himself who is the Son of God, and our everlasting High Priest, build you up in faith and truth, and in all meekness, patience, long-suffering, forbearance, and purity; and may He bestow on you a lot and portion among His Saints, and on us with you, and on all that are under heaven, who shall believe in our Lord Jesus

Christ, and in His Father, who "raised Him from the dead." Pray for all the saints. Pray also for kings, and rulers, and princes, and for those that persecute and hate you, and for the enemies of the cross, that your fruits may be manifest to all, and that ye may be perfect in Him.

The Martyrdom of Polycarp
Encyclical Epistle of the Church of Smyrna (150 A.D.)
Chapter 1
Subject of Which We Write

We have written to you, brethren, as to what relates to the martyrs, and especially to the blessed Polycarp, who put an end to the persecution, having, as it were, set a seal upon it by his martyrdom. For almost all the events that happened previously to this one took place that the Lord might show us from above a martyrdom becoming the Gospel. For he waited to be delivered up, even as the Lord has done, that we also might become his followers, while we look not merely at what concerns ourselves, but have regard also to our neighbors. For it is the part of a true and well-founded love, not only to wish one's self to be saved, but also all the brethren.

Chapter IX
Polycarp Refuses to Revile Christ

Now, as Polycarp was entering into the stadium, there came to him a voice from heaven saying, "Be strong, and show thyself a man, O Polycarp!" No one saw who that spoke to him; but those of our brethren who were present heard the voice. And as he was brought forward, the commotion became great when they heard that Polycarp was taken. And when he came near, the proconsul asked him whether he was Polycarp. On his confession that he was, they sought to persuade him to deny Christ, saying, "Have respect to thy old age" and other similar things, according to their custom, such as "Swear by the fortune of Caesar; repent and say, Away with the Atheists." But Polycarp, gazing with a stern countenance on all the multitude of the wicked heathen then in the stadium, and waving his hand towards them, while with groans he looked up to heaven, said, "Away with Atheists." Then, the proconsul urged him, saying, "Swear, and I will set thee at liberty, reproach Christ." Polycarp declared, "Eighty and six years have I served Him, and He never did me any injury: how then can I blaspheme my King and my Savior?"

Chapter XI
No Threats Have Any Effect
The proconsul then said to him, "I have wild beasts at hand; to these will I cast thee, except thou repent." But he answered, "Call them then, for we are not accustomed to repent of what is good in order to adopt that which is evil; and it is well for me to be changed from what is evil to what is righteous." But again the proconsul said to him, "I will cause thee to be consumed by fire, seeing thou despiseth wild beasts, if thou will not repent." But Polycarp said, "Thou threatenest me with fire, which burneth for an hour, and after a little is extinguished, but are ignorant of the fire of the coming judgment and of eternal punishment, reserved for the ungodly. But why linger thou? Bring forth what thou wilt."

Chapter XV
Polycarp Is Not Injured by the Fire
When he had pronounced this amen and so finished his prayer, those who were appointed for the purpose kindled the fire. And as the flame blazed forth in great fury, we, to whom it was given to witness it, beheld a great miracle, and have been preserved that we might report to others what then took place. For the fire, shaping itself into the form of an arch, like the sail of a ship when filled with the wind, encompassed as by a circle the body of the martyr. And he appeared within not like flesh which is burnt, but as bread is baked, or so as gold and silver glowing in a furnace. Moreover, we perceived such a sweet odor coming

from the pile, as if frankincense or some such precious spices had been smoking there.

Chapter VI
Polycarp Is Pierced by a Dagger

At length, when those wicked men perceived that his body could not be consumed by the fire, they commanded an executioner to tear and pierce him through with a dagger. And on his doing this, there came forth a dove, and a great quantity of blood, so that the fire was extinguished; and all the people wondered that there should be such a difference between the unbelievers and the elect, of whom this most admirable Polycarp was one, having in our times been an apostolic and prophetic teacher, and Bishop of the Catholic Church which is in Smyrna. For every word that went out of his mouth either has been or shall yet be done.

Chapter XVII
The Christians Are Refused Polycarp's Body

But when the adversary of the race of the righteous, the envious, malicious, and wicked one, perceived the impressive nature of his martyrdom and considered the blameless life he had led from the beginning, and how he was not crowned with the wreath of immortality, having beyond dispute received his rewards, he did his utmost that not the least memorial of him should be taken away by us, although many desired to do this, and to become possessors of his holy flesh. For this end he suggested it to Nicetes, the father of Herod and brother of Alce, to go and entrust the governor not to give up his body to buried, "Lest," said he, "forsaking Him that was crucified, they begin to worship this one." This he said at the suggestion and persuasion of the Jews, who also watched us, as we sought to take him out of the fire, being ignorant of this, that it is neither possible for us ever to forsake Christ, who suffered for the salvation of such as shall be saved throughout the whole world, the blameless one for sinners, nor to worship any other. For Him indeed, as being the Son of God, we adore; but the martyrs, as disciples and followers of the Lord, we worthily love on account of their extraordinary affection towards their own King and Master, of whom may we also be made companions and fellow-disciples.

Chapter XIV
Praise the Martyr Polycarp

This, then, is the account of the blessed Polycarp, who being the twelfth that was martyred in Smyrna (reckoning those also of Philadelphia), yet occupies a place of his own in the memory of all men, insomuch that he is everywhere spoken of by the heathen themselves. He was not merely an illustrious teacher, but also a pre-eminent martyr, whose martyrdom all desire to imitate, as having been altogether consistent with the Gospel of Christ. For, having through patience overcome the unjust governor, and thus acquired the crown of immortality, he now, with the Apostles and all the righteous in heaven, rejoicingly glorifies God, even the Father, and our Lord Jesus Christ, the Savior of our souls, the Governor of our bodies, and the Shepherd of the Catholic Church throughout the world.

Justin Martyr (100-163 or 167)

He was a professional philosopher, who traveled from place to place, lecturing on Christianity. He opened a school of philosophy in Rome, and later was beheaded for refusing to sacrifice to the pagan gods. Justin Martyr was the first layman to have written on Christianity at any length. Two of his most important works are still extant: the *Apologies* and the *Dialogue with Trypho.*

Justin, in his first "Apology," begins by refuting the accusations raised against the Christians and presents and justifies the contents of their religion. Attention is given to worship and the fullest description which is from the Sacraments of Baptism and the Eucharist.

> And this food is called the Eucharist of which no one is allowed to partake, but the man who believes that the thing which is for the remission of sins, and unto regeneration and who is so living in Christ has enjoyed. For not as common bread and common drink do we receive these; but in like manner as Jesus Christ our Savior, having been made flesh by the words of God, had both flesh and blood for our salvation; so likewise have we been taught that the food which is blessed by the prayer of His word, and from which or blood and flesh by transmutation are nourished, is the flesh and blood of that Jesus Who made flesh.

In Justin's letter to Trypho, it is intended to appeal to the members of the Old Israel and to present Jesus to them as the fulfiller of the Law.

Irenaeus (125-203)
Bishop of Lyons in Gaul

Born in Asia Minor, Irenaeus was well educated, and he knew and was taught by men who knew the Apostles, such as Polycarp, a pupil of John the Apostle. In 178 A.D., he became Bishop in Lyons. Irenaeus was the first great Christian theologian. His treatise is witness to the Apostolic tradition and the primacy of the Pope. His principle writings were "Against the Heresies," in 180 A.D.

Against the Heresies

The churches which have been planted in Germany
do not believe or hand down anything different, nor
do those in Spain, nor do those in Gaul, nor those
which have been established in the central regions.

Irenaeus is saying that the teachings and doctrines taught by the Apostles are the same all over: universal, Catholic, as are being taught in his day. The writings of such men as Irenaeus, who was world-famous and died a martyr in 203 A.D. for his faith, is as reliable testimony from historic antiquity as can be found of the teachings and traditions handed down to us by the Apostles.

Irenaeus also speaks of the Eucharist:

As the bread which is produced from the earth when
it receives the invocation of God is no more
common bread, but the Eucharist, consisting of two
realities, earthly and Heavenly, so also our bodies,
when they receive the Eucharist are no longer
corruptible, having the hope of the resurrection to
eternity....

Eusebius of Caesarea (260-340 A.D.)

Eusebius' works are the "Church History from A.D. 1 to 324," consisting of ten books written in Greek which are still extant. After completing these ten books, he writes, "The Life of Constantine." Eusebius lived during the great persecution of Diocletian, which broke out in 303 A.D. Not long after the persecution, he became Bishop of Caesarea of Palestine. Eusebius collected many sources of knowledge that are no longer known to us. But even though they are lost, these documents, which he quotes, have given researchers a more extensive look into the history of the early Church. Jerome writes, "Eusebius, Bishop of Caesarea in Palestine, a man most studious in the Scripture, and along with Pamhilus the Martyr a most diligent investigator of sacred literature, has edited an infinite number of volumes." After his completion of Church history, Eusebius would go on to record in writing the proceedings of the first worldwide council of the Universal Church since the days of the Apostles. This council was to proclaim the unity of the Church and its religious ideas. He writes as a historian of the present day would write, for the information and instruction of his contemporaries and of those who should come after. His plan is stated at the very beginning of his works:

> It is my purpose to write on account of the succession of the Holy Apostles, as well as the time which has elapsed from the days of our Savior to our own; and to relate the important events are said to have occurred in the history of the Church....It is my purpose also to give the names and number and the times of those who through love of innovation have run in the greatest errors, and proclaiming themselves discoverers of knowledge, falsely so-called have, like fierce wolves, unmercifully devastated the flock of Christ.

Church History, Book II, Chapter XXV
Peter and Paul Martyred at Rome

When the government of Nero was now firmly established, he began to plunge into unholy pursuit, and armed himself even against the religion of God of the universe. To describe the greatness of his depravity does not lie within the plan of the present work. As there are many indeed that have recorded Nero's history in most accurate narratives, everyone may at his leisure learn from them the coarseness of the man's extraordinary madness that accomplished the destruction of so many without any reason. He ran into such blood guilt lines that he did not spare even his nearest relatives and dearest friends, but destroyed his mother and brothers and wife, with very many others of his family as he would private and public enemies, with various kinds of deaths. But with all these things this particular in the catalogue of his crimes was still wanting, that he was the first of the emperors who showed himself an enemy of the divine religion. The Roman Tertullian is likewise a witness of this. He writes as follows: "Examine your records. There you will find that Nero was the first that persecuted this doctrine, particularly when after subduing all the east, he exercised his cruelty against all Rome. We glory in having such a man the leader in our punishment, for whoever was condemned by Nero unless it was something of great excellence. Thus publicly announcing himself as the first among God's chief enemies, he was led on to the slaughter of the Apostles. It is therefore recorded that Paul was beheaded in Rome itself, and that Peter was likewise crucified under Nero. This account of Peter and Paul is substantiated by the fact that their names are preserved in the cemeteries of that place even to the present day. It is confirmed by Caius, a member of the Church, who arose under Zephyrinus, Bishop of Rome, He, in a published disputation with Proclus, the leader of the Phrygian heresy, speaks as follows concerning the place where the sacred corpses of the Apostles are laid: "But I can show the trophies of the Apostles. For if you will go to the Vatican or to the Astisan way, you will find the trophies of those who laid the foundations of the Church." And that they both suffered martyrdom at the same time is stated by Dionysius, Bishop of Corinth, in his "Epistle to the Romans," in the following words: "You have thus by such an admonition bound together the planting of Peter and of Paul at Rome and Corinth, for both of them planted and likewise taught us in our Corinth. And they taught together in the like manner in Italy, and suffered martyrdom at the same time." I have quoted these things in order that the truth of the history might be still more confirmed.

Life of Constantine, Book III, Chapter VII
Of the General Council, at Which Bishops from
All Nations Were Present

In effect, the most distinguished of God's ministers from all the churches which abounded in Europe, Lybia, (Africa) and Asia were assembled. And a single house of prayer, as though divinely enlarged, sufficed to contain at once Syrians and Clicians, Phoenicians and Arabians, delegates from Palestine, and others from Egypt; Thebans and Libyans, with those who came from regions of Mesopotamia. A Persian Bishop, too, was present at this conference; nor was even a Scythian found wanting among the numbers of foreign and missionary bishops....Even from Spain itself, one assembly. The prelate of the imperial city was prevented from attending by extreme old age; but his presbyters were present and supplied his garland as this with the bond of peace, and presented it to his Savior as a thank-offering for the victories he had sustained over every foe, thus exhibiting in our own time a similitude of the Apostolic company.

Chapter XII
Constantine's Address to the Council Concerning Peace

It was once my chief desire, dearest friends, to enjoy the spectacle of your united presence; and now that this desire is fulfilled, I feel myself bound to render thanks to God the universal King, because, in addition to all His other benefits, He has granted me a blessing that all the rest, in permitting me to see you not only all assembled together, but all united in a common harmony of sentiment. I pray therefore that no malignant adversary may henceforth interfere to mar our happy state; I pray that, now the impious hostility of the tyrants had been forever removed by the power of God our Savior, that spirit who delights in the evil may devise no other means for exposing the divine law to blasphemous calamity; for, in my judgment, intestine strife within the Church of God is far more evil and dangerous than any kind of war or conflict; and these our differences appear to me more grievous than any outward trouble. Accordingly, when, by the will and with the cooperation of God, I had been victorious over my enemies, I though that nothing more remained but to render thanks to Him, and sympathize in the joy of those whom He had restored to freedom through my instrumentality; as soon as I heard that intelligence which I had least expected to receive, I mean the news of your dissension, I judged it to be of no secondary importance, but with the earnest desire that a remedy for this evil also might be found through my means, I immediately sent to require your presence. And now I rejoice in beholding your assembly; but I feel that my desire will be most completely fulfilled when I can see you all united in one judgment, and that common spirit of peace and concord prevailing amongst you, which it becomes you as consecrated to the service of God, to commend to others. Delay not then, dear friends: delay not, ye ministers of God, and faithful servants of Him who is our Lord and Savior: begin from this moment to discard the cause of that disunion which has existed among you, and remove the perplexities of controversy by embracing the principles of peace. For by such conduct you will at the same time be acting in a manner most pleasing to the supreme God, and you will confer an exceeding favor on me who am your fellow servant.

Augustine of Hippo (354-430 A.D.)

Augustine was the dominant figure in the African Churches. He is well known for his spiritual writings including hundreds of sermons, and letters which are still read and studied today. Among his best known works are his *Confessions* and *The City of God.* Augustine is considered one of the greatest of the Fathers and Doctors of the Church.

Contained in Augustine's writings, (Book One on Christian doctrine), he shows that love, the love of God for His own sake and the love of our neighbor for God's sake is the fulfillment and the end of all Scripture.

On Christian Doctrine, Book I, Chapter XXVI
The Command to Love God And Our Neighbor
Includes a Command to Love Ourselves

Seeing, then, that there is no need of a command that every man should love himself and his own body, seeing, that is, that we love ourselves, and what is beneath us but connected with us, through a law of nature which has never been violated and which is common to us with the beasts (for even the beasts love themselves and their own bodies), it only remained necessary to lay injunctions upon us in regard to God above us, and our neighbor beside us. "Thou shalt love," he says, "the Lord thy God with all thy heart, and with all thy soul, and with all thy mind; and thou shalt love thy neighbor as thyself. On these two commandments hang all the law and the prophets." Thus the end of the commandments is love, and that twofold, the love of God and the love of our neighbor. Nor, if you take yourself in your entirety, that is, soul and body together, and your neighbor in his entirety, soul and body together (for man is made up of soul and body together), you will find that none of the classes of things that are to be loved is over liked in these two commandments. For though, when the love of God comes first, and the measure of our love for Him is prescribed in such terms that it is evident all other things are to find their center in Him, nothing seems to be said about our love for ourselves; yet when it is said, "Thou shalt love thy neighbor as thyself," it at once becomes evident that our love for ourselves has not been overlooked.

Chapter XXVII
The Order of Love

Now he is a man of just and holy life who forms an unprejudiced estimate of things, and keeps his affections also under strict control, so that he neither loves what he ought not to love, nor fails to love what he ought to love, nor loves that more which ought to be loved less, nor loves that equally which ought to be loved either less or more, nor loves that less or more which ought to be loved equally. No sinner is to be loved as a sinner; and every man is to be loved as a man for God's sake; but God is to be loved for His own sake. And if God is to be loved more than any man, each man ought to love God more than himself. Likewise, we ought to love another man better than our own body, because all things are to be loved in reference to God, and another man can have fellowship with us in the enjoyment of God, whereas our body cannot; for the body only lives through the soul, and it is by the soul that we enjoy God.

Chapter XXX
Are Angels to be Reckoned as Neighbors?

There arises further in this connection a question about angels. For they are happy in the enjoyment of Him whom we long to enjoy; and the more we enjoy Him in this life as through a glass darkly, the more easy do we find it to bear our pilgrimage, and the more eagerly do we long for its termination. But it is not irrational to ask whether in love of angels also. For that He who commanded us to love our neighbor made no exception, as far as men are concerned, is shown both by our Lord Himself in the Gospel, and by the Apostle Paul. For when the man to whom our

Lord delivered those two commandments, and to whom He said that on these hang all the law and the prophets, asked Him, "And who is my neighbor," He told him of a certain man who, going down from Jerusalem to Jericho, fell among thieves, and was severely wounded by them, and left naked and half dead. And He showed him that nobody was neighbor to this man except him who took pity upon him and came forward to relieve and care for him. And the man who had asked the question admitted the truth of this when he was himself interrogated in turn. To whom our Lord says, "Go and do thou likewise," teaching us that he is our neighbor whom it is our duty to help in his need or whom it would be our duty to help if he were in need, whence it follows, that he whose duty it would be in turn to help us is our neighbor. For the name "neighbor" is a relative one, and no one can be neighbor except to a neighbor. And, again, who does not see a person to whom the office of mercy may be denied when our Lord extends the rule even to our enemies? "Love your enemies, do good to them that hate you."

And so also the Apostle Paul teaches when he says: "For this, Thou shalt not commit adultery, Thou shalt not kill, Thou shalt not steal, Thou shalt not bear false witness, Thou shalt not covet; and if there by any other commandments, it is briefly comprehended in this saying namely, "Thou shalt love thy neighbor as thyself. Love worketh no ill to his neighbor." Whosoever then supposes that the Apostle did not embrace every man is at once absurd and most pernicious. The Apostle thought it a sin, if a man were not a Christian or were an enemy, to commit adultery with his wife, or to kill him, or to covet his goods. And as nobody but a fool would say this, it is clear that every man is to be considered our neighbor because we are to work no ill to any man.

But now, if everyone to whom we ought to show, or who ought to show us, the office of mercy is by right called a neighbor, it is manifest that the command to love our neighbor embraces the holy Angels also, seeing that so great offices of mercy have been performed by them on our behalf, as may easily be shown by turning the attention to many passages of Holy Scripture. And on this ground even God Himself, our Lord, desired to be called our neighbor. For our Lord Jesus Christ points to Himself under the figure of a man who brought aid to him who was lying half dead on the road, wounded and abandoned by the robbers. And the Psalmist says in his prayer, "I behave myself as though he had been my friend or brother." But as the divine nature is of higher excellence than, and far removed above, our nature, the command to love God is distinct from that to love our neighbor. For He shows us pity on account of His own goodness, but we show pity to one another on account of His; that is, He pities us that we may fully enjoy Himself; we pity one another that we may fully enjoy Him.

Chapter XXXVI
The Interpretation of Scripture

Whoever, then, thinks that he understands the Holy Scriptures, or any part of them, but puts such an interpretation upon them as does not tend to build up this twofold love of God and our neighbor, does not yet understand them as he ought. If, on the other hand, a man draws a meaning from them that may be used for the building up of love, even though he does not happen upon the precise meaning which the author whom he reads intended to express in that place, his error is not pernicious, and he is wholly clear from the charge of deception. From there is involved in deception the intention to say what is false; and we find plenty of people who intended to deceive, but nobody who wishes to be deceived. Since, then, the man who knows practices deceit, and the ignorant man is practiced upon, it is quite clear that in any particular case the man who is deceived is a better man than the man who deceives, seeing that it is better to suffer than to commit injustice. Now every man who lies commits an injustice; and if any man thinks that a lie is ever useful, he must think that injustice is sometimes useful. For no liar keeps faith in the matter about which he lies. He wishes, of course, that the man to whom he lies should place confidence in him; and yet he betrays his confidence by lying to him. Now every man who breaks faith is unjust. Either, then, injustice is sometimes useful (which is impossible), or a lie is never useful.

Whoever takes another meaning out of Scripture than the writer intended, goes astray, but not through any falsehood in Scripture. Nevertheless, as I was going to say, if his mistaken interpretation tends to build up love, which is the end of the commandments, he goes astray in much the same way as a man who by mistake quits the high road, but yet reaches through the fields the same place to which the road leads. He is to be corrected, however, and to be shown how much better it is not to quit the straight road, lest he even go in the wrong direction altogether.

Chapter XXXVII
Dangers of Mistaken Interpretation

For if he takes up rashly a meaning which the author whom he is reading did not intend, he often falls in with other statements which he cannot harmonize with this meaning. And if he admits that these statements are true and certain, then it follows that the meaning he had put upon the former passage cannot be the true one: and so it comes to pass, one can hardly tell how, that, out of love for his own opinion, he begins to feel more angry with Scripture than he is with himself. And if he should once permit that evil to creep in, it will utterly destroy him. "For we walk by faith, not sight." Now faith will totter, love itself will grow cold. For if a man has fallen from faith, he must necessarily also fall from love; for he cannot love what he does not believe to exist. But if he both believes and loves, then through good works, and through diligent attention to the precepts of morality, he comes to hope also that he shall attain the object of his love. And so these are the three things to which all knowledge and all prophecy are subservient: Faith, Hope, Love.

The Writings of the Early Church Fathers is a 38-volume set, published by Wm. B. Eerdmans, Publishing Co., Grand Rapids, Michigan.

INDEX